Squish Art

An Imagination Tool

Color Method for
Fostering Society's Newest Orphan,
Creativity

Experienced, Written, Edited & Typeset

by

Hod Doering

Third Edition, November 2009
Expanded text plus demonstration photos

The Poetry Barn
Graytown, Ohio
USA

Poetry chapbooks by Hod from The Poetry Barn:

Hod's Family Albumin — A sort of Celebration of family in Several Parts; limited private edition

The Nothing and Beingness series: Summer Seasonings; Fall Seasonings; Winter Seasonings; Spring Seasonings; The I Don't Care Bears Club

Notes on Love at 44 & 21 — An Extended Valentine

Scrivener In The Lobby — Poems noted at The Lobby Coffee House, Toledo, Ohio

Moments Before Death — A Cerebration On Life

Adventures Of Brandon Butterfly

Conceived On A Submarine — Poems noted at The Original Sub Shop & Deli, Toledo, Ohio

Big O Poems

Family Album

Margotiations — Poems noted at Andy's Jazz Club, Chicago, Illinois

Five Dead Junkies Whose Names I Never Knew

Perfectbound Poetry Books by Hod:

Seven Pack #1: Things Your parents should have told you in the beginning

Seven Pack #2: Poetry in E and Pro motion

Seven Pack #3: Odd Me in Poet-Tree

Look for Hod's 8-pagers, short poem books, 90 titles so far:

A for Aspiration, Argument & Art, About Poems 1, About Poems 2, As Charged, B is for Bad & Badinage, Badditude, Blues Take 1, Blues Take 2, C is for Commune Chaos & Calumny, D is for Dead, E is for Everything, F is for Funny Friendship Failure, Farewell Charlotte, Fathers & Songs, For Betty, Funeral Flowers, G is for Good, Gentle & Green, H is for Hands, Hair Deal, Heinous acts on days of Infamy, Hive Of Never Bees, I is for Inspiration Intuition Insides, J is for Jakki, Jake, K is for Kiss Karma & Kill, L is for Love & Lust, L2 Equals Love * Lust, Lobbraray, Lost Inside My Raingelfish, Lost Nearly Poems, M-Alpha, Me Poems 1, Me Poems 2, Me Poems 3, Me Poems 4, Millennial Poem Accidents (D), My Media Mixer, My Media Mixer a, My Rules, N is for Not & Never, O is for Old & Oh My, O2 is for Oxygen & Other Oddities, O3-Alpha, Odd Poems1, Odd Poems 2, Odd Poems 3, One Family, Only I Owe You, Only poems, Or And Butgasms, Orgasm Litanies, P-Alpha, People You Almost Meet, Q-Alpha, Questions 1, Questions 2, R-Alpha, Relations, S-Alpha, S2-Alpha, Sex Buttons I never Wore, Sex Sells, Seven Strong Serving Men, Share My Shorts, Share My Shorts 2, Simple Pleasures, Stones, Miles & Smiles, Stupididity, T is For Truth, Tai Cheating Life, Tai Cheating Life, Too, Teachers Who/Whon't (D), Teaching Learning Poetry , The Trail, Thousand Poem Party , Too Family, Truth Strangers, True-Truth Lies, U is for Un, U is for Unto Too, V Is For Vanity, Vision & Vanilla, W Is For wRong, Walk An Hour In My Mind, Xmas Seasonings, Xmas Stories, Xmas Stories/Xmas Seasonings (D), You Could Be A Poet, You Might Be A Poet, You Might Be A Poet/Could Be A Poet (D)

Humor: Yard Geese Police Task Force "Ticket Book"

Textbook: Thinker's Journey into How to Think and Solve Problems – A basic thinking manual

This book is dedicated to my grandchildren (In order of appearance): Bailey, Foster, Aubrey, and Ellie in hope that their regeneration will be somehow better than mine/ours; in hope that they will be able to do a little more good.

Preface

I have successfully used the techniques presented in this book for over fifteen years now with life units ranging from two to seventy years of age to create lasting art and inspire creative and pleasurable moments in homes and in workshops.

Originally borrowed from kindergarten fingerpainting, these techniques have been enhanced by trial and error and input from family, friends and workshopped experience, filtered through and by me to become a system for presenting, enhancing and enjoying the creative process.

Squish Art is enjoyable on its own, but it can also become the basis or lead-in for creative writing and thinking in both home and school.

This is the spirit and hope that has inspired me to offer this system to you in this book and to continue to promote this on my own with workshops across the country as well as to pursue it as an art form myself. I have used the techniques presented here to create several hundred works of abstract art and over 12,000 poems.

I hope you can find yourself in your art as I have and that you share both with the world. If my work can assist you in that process then I am pleased as well as honored and humbled.

Yours in art and creativity,
Hod Doering
November 2009

Book Note

This is meant to be a working book for everyday use, not a coffee table book to be dusted and ignored. With that in mind, to save you money and thereby promote wider distribution of the ideas and concepts presented here, I have made all the illustrations inside the book black and white or grayscale. This is because with this current publishing system and company it is considerably more expensive to print a book if any pages are in color. We can hope that this changes soon.

If I find that there is demand it is possible to publish a color version, but at roughly double the B&W cover price.

If you would like to see the art in color
(of course you do!)
please email me at squishart@gmail.com
with colorart in the subject line
and I will send you the color versions
of the works used in this book.

Table of Contents

Poems
And
Illustrations

All photos by Patty

Introductions

Poetry Production Lines

I have written over 12,800 poems in a little over twenty years. Many of these are good, a small percentage are excellent. All of them are competent works. In 2009 I wrote over one thousand poems in six months. Not bragging . . . much, just a fact. I would like to share with you some of the techniques I have found useful to keep up the flow of ideas and words leading to poems.

First you need to read and to have read the works of other poets and writers. For several decades I have attempted, with some success, to read the entire works of one famous poet per year. I attend local poetry events and readings once or twice per month. I get to regional and national events as often as time and money can afford; about one every three years has been my average over the last two decades.

I also suggest you experience art and music; dance however you may be able. Following that you need to see the world. See with eyes and ears, hands and skin. Experience your self and this strange world around you.

Organization seems to me to be the toughest part of writing efficiency. In fact some poets seem to revel in their lack of efficiency. You need to get a place to write. Yes, you can write and should write, or at least take notes anywhere anytime. But you need an official place to finalize your work into poems and stories. My spouse has been kind enough to allow me a small room with a large computer for this purpose.

Another important component is time. If you don't have to make time you may not be out experiencing life and the world around you. Some poets or writers schedule this time on a daily or weekly basis. For example, I read of one successful writer who wrote every weekday for two hours immediately after dinner regardless of how he felt or what ideas might be stewing inside his head. This worked for him. Another poet who has made it and is earning a living at his writing already said he goes out into his garden at his estate on Maui to muse and write for several hours every morning. Maybe after retirement?

I have developed a different set of rules. I write whenever I can get the time. Most weeks I try to get at least ten hours in, but I don't get upset if I get one or twenty hours in. I have, instead of worrying about regimenting my time, managed to streamline my process.

I journal fairly regularly, keeping more of an idea journal than a story or reporting journal. I carry small notebooks and pens to record these thoughts and ideas at all times when I am out of the house. In the house I have reams of paper ready to record things as they occur. I used to keep paper and pen beside my bed to record things, but, for now, the computer is in the next room and I use it. Every month or so I take all these notes and copy them into a bigger, hardbound journal.

Whenever I get a few minutes to myself I open up my word processor and create fifteen or thirty blank documents from my poem template. The template merely holds the line and font formats which I have decided to make standard.

I then open up one or more of my idea journals and type in an idea from there (idea pebbles, if you will. See that section later in this book) into each blank template. These poem-ready candies are then prepared to be activated at a moment's notice whenever I can garner a minute or ten to create new poems.

For me this process has eliminated those blank-page blues and maximized my poetry writing time. One major idea generation assistant is the Squish Art creativity process detailed in this book. I hope you enjoy Squishing and that your creative productivity goes up as mine has.

Where To Begin: How About Here?

Creativity is one of the essentials for human happiness. Although not actually named as one of the five basic needs by Maslow:

Biological and Physiological needs - air, food, drink, shelter, warmth, sex, sleep, etc.

Safety needs - protection from elements, security, order, law, limits, stability, etc.

Belongingness and Love needs - work group, family, affection, relationships, etc.

Esteem needs - self-esteem, achievement, mastery, independence, status, dominance, prestige, managerial responsibility, etc.

Self-Actualization needs - realizing personal potential, self-fulfillment, seeking personal growth and peak experiences.

I feel that Creative release and satisfaction falls under one or both of categories 4 and 5 in the above list. I know that the creative process keeps me relatively sane.

Where are the lines?

Staying inside the lines is good! We all learned that in grade school.
Staying inside the lines is bad! — it stifles creativity. And other sayings
opening dissimilar veins we've all heard from more than two sides.

It may surprise you to know that I agree with both, partly. It is nice to
be able to stay inside the lines. We also should know how to color
outside the lines, when to add, delete or make up our own lines. This
applies far beyond the bounds of coloring book pages.

In art, and in life, we need to be able to make up our own lines to color in
or out of. We need to be able to operate where there are no lines. We
need to be able to be beyond lines, to let go of being controlled without
losing our control, to exert control when necessary, to be able to let
control loose. So . . .

Shall we Squish?

Big Bang 1992:

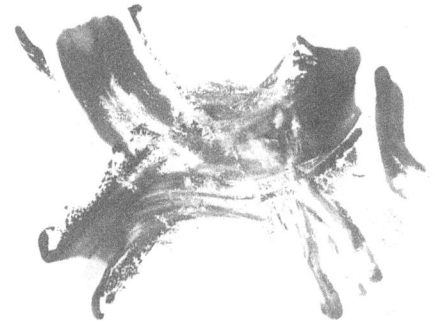

Is This Art?

Art without serious intent is fruitless, momentary.
Art without lightness of spirit is ponderous, joyless.
Squish Art is real art.
Squish Art is fun art.
Squish Art shouldn't be taken too seriously.
Squish Art should not be taken too lightly.

Squish Art should be taken often
in generous doses.

Rainbow People 1993

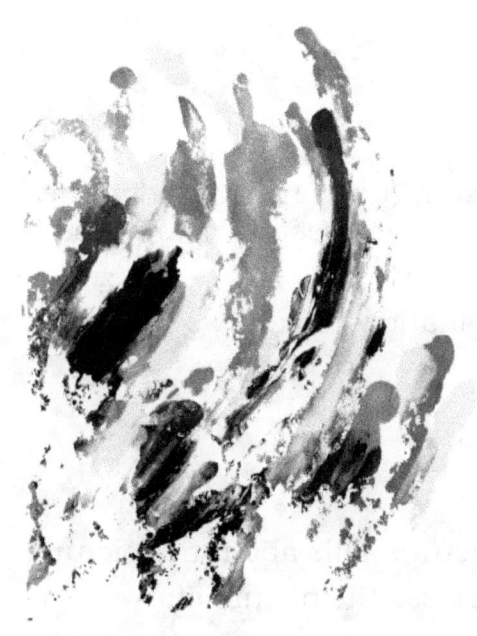

Wherefrom art though Squish Art?

Squish Art evolved in our house, on our dining room table directly from fingerpainting. I originally wanted to achieve a lasting effect similar to the transitory one which the relatively cheap and flaky fingerpaints could only hold for a few days.

As techniques grew and varied so did depth of purpose and application of Squishing pictures. Pictures hold stories. Abstract pictures hold nothing. Abstract pictures hold everything. Every-any story may be hidden there like your personality behind inkblots where you never thought to look.

Many people have noted the similarity to the Rorschach tests used by Psychologists although the vividness of artist quality color paint lends itself much more to imagination stimulation and creates permanent art in addition to allowing your crazy person to shout out. It was only a short step from having fun creating art to having more fun naming each picture and telling its story.

Not surprisingly, each viewer can, and often does, come up with a different picture story or even a different picture since the picture or pictures seen in a particular Squish exist in the eye and mind of the viewer; the art itself is only a suggestion of a suggestion of an idea.

This is the heart of Squish Art, the Imagination Tool:

1)   Create a picture painting.
2)   Find a picture story inside.
3)   Find a name for that picture story.
4)   Make up a story which tells the picture, tells about the picture.
5)   Write a poem or short story which uses the picture story.
6)   Place them together on your wall, in your heart, in your mind.

Then go back and turn the picture other directions, ways, or times to find more stories. Share picture story-names-poems. Debate their relative merits. Defend your own. Defend someone else's!

8

Getting Ready

Before You Start – The Paints

Squish Art works best with artist quality acrylic paint. To start choose bright rainbow colors plus black and white if you can afford it. Add a brown or two next month. How about a grey? Textured gesso? Metallic sheen colors?

I use and recommend Liquitex Acrylic Artist Color from Binney & Smith, either in medium or heavy body consistency. Binney & Smith added a cheaper, more watery paint in 2000 or so under the name Basics® which is available many places. I feel that this does not work well for Squish Art because of its lighter consistency, but you may have your own experience so feel free to experiment and have fun. I have not yet found any bargain, variety store acrylics that gave satisfactory service and have pretty much stopped looking. Binney & Smith markets starter assortments in 3/4 oz (6) tubes, #1070 (Several starter kits from $25 to $50 are available online at www.artsuppliesonline.com) and 2 oz (6) tubes, #1037 (in my opinion, a better value at $31). Either is a good way to start, but #1070 does not include black and white. Later, you may wish to buy different individual hues. I have accumulated a lot of different colors over the last decade or so, but you can premix your own if you like. (These are 2008, Ohio prices & products. See Resources for more info.)

Read safety directions and warnings on all paints carefully!!

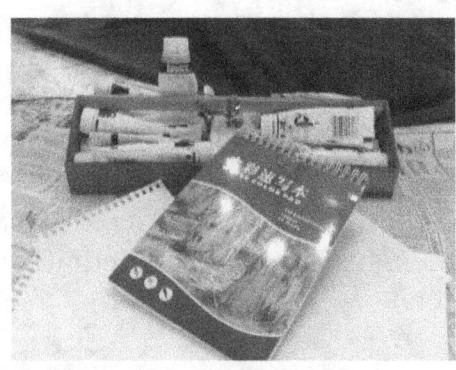

While acrylics are safe for all ages some few acrylic paints do contain toxic substances. These paints are not suitable for children who might put them in their mouth, eyes, etc. Contact your retailer or the manufacturer for details.

•• Children should be supervised ••

This is a good working kit

Here is some information from the Liquitex web page which I found interesting concerning their paints.

(From http://www.liquitex.com/resources/faq.cfm June 2008)

"Liquitex Acrylic Paints, Mediums and Varnishes are water based (and water clean up). There are no fumes associated with using Liquitex other than a slight ammonia smell. All Liquitex products are labeled "AP Non-Toxic" by The Art and Creative Materials Institute with the exception of the following: Cadmium Colors - Do not spray apply / Liquitex Soluvar Varnish - contains Mineral Spirits.

"Toxicologists at the Art and Creative Materials Institute have been certifying safety and quality in art materials since 1940. New Liquitex labels use the AP symbol to indicate Non-Toxic but the phrase "Non-Toxic" has been removed due to European labeling standards. Liquitex products are also labeled for California Prop. 65 which requires that any trace amount (no matter how small) of a toxic substance appear on the label.

For more information you can contact the ACMI directly (See Bibliography):

"There is no natural latex used in Liquitex products. In fact, the only products ColArt (Liquitex parent company) manufactures containing rubber latex are Art Masking Fluid and Colorless Art Masking Fluid. Both these products are labeled for possible allergic reaction. There is no formaldehyde, peanut oil, dairy products, egg or wheat products used in Liquitex products.

All Liquitex colors have been TCLP analyzed for RCRA 8 metals. The colors that exceeded EPA solubility limits for chromium are: Cobalt Green and Cobalt Turquoise. With the exception of the Cadmium colors (Cadmium "Hue" colors are OK), Cobalt Green and Cobalt Turquoise, the entire line of colors is safe for use by children or in a child's room."

Clean up any spills or swipes on skin or clothes, or furniture immediately with soap and water.

Before You Start – The Work Area

Dedicate a roll of paper towels to the art area. Keep a wet paper towel on hand as you work. Change as needed. Wear old clothes. Use a smock or dedicated work shirt. Always use protective layers of newsprint or other throwaway paper to completely cover work areas. Acrylic on skin will wear off in a day or three. However, it is permanent, once dried, on furniture, floors, clothes, drapes, carpet, etc and must be scraped off.

ARTIST'S ACRYLIC PAINTS
are
PERMANENT WHEN DRY

Clean up any paint spills or swipes on skin or clothes, etc. immediately with soap and water.

Children, especially young children, should be carefully supervised. Some paints contain potentially toxic ingredients. See "Before You Start – The Paints."

•• Children should be supervised ••

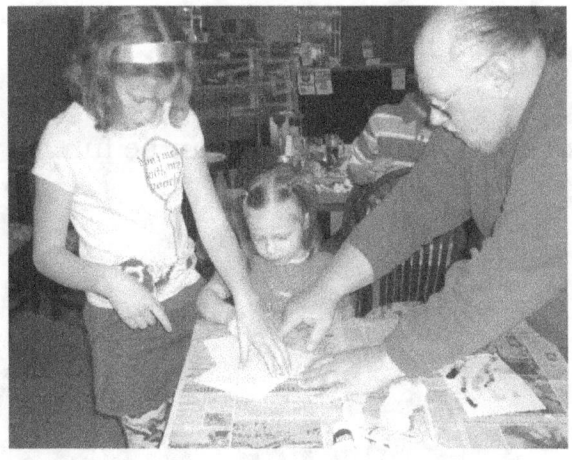

Ellie's First Squish

Before You Start – Paper

Always use acid-free, quality art paper for Squish Art. Cheap paper not only tears easily, it wrinkles and will not hold its shape. I suggest 70lb, or heavier, acid free artist's paper. Heavy drawing paper is ok, but I prefer watercolor paper as this seems to work better for me.   I mostly use 140lb Watercolor paper nowadays. I find this works especially well for larger paper sizes.

I recommend starting with relatively small, 6"x9" pieces (a 9"x12" standard size sheet cut in half) of 70-80 pound drawing paper for both economy and control. This also allows many more squishes from your basic paint set. Find any paper which you enjoy working with and use that. Check prices in your area for watercolor papers. You may find that you can get smaller watercolor papers at or near the same price as heavier drawing paper. Experiment to find what you like.

Paper size used for any given work depends on the individual artist and the work to be presented or represented. Once you feel comfortable with the techniques and results of Squishing feel free to try larger paper and different color papers to create many different effects. Invade your local art supplies store and see what they have waiting for you.

I most often use 140lb archival/artist quality watercolor paper for my personal work.

Work safely. Have fun. Art can be fun.
Fun is an art.
Take your fun seriously.

Before You Start – Resources

Anything which is not fun is not worth taking seriously. — Frank Lloyd Wright in response to criticism that his architecture was only fun, not serious, architecture. What? You never heard of him. Look him up.

Build your knowledge; expand your horizons. Paint them eccentrically.

You can find artist's acrylic paint and paper at your local art supply store. If they do not stock Liquitex brand you can call or write to the National Art Materials Trade Association for a dealer near you (See Bibliography).

Also look on the web at www.Liquitex.com. Go to the website for many ideas and tips using their product. Also ask your art supply dealer for literature by Binney & Smith (Liquitex or ColArt Americas – Liquitex's new distributor. See Bibliography) concerning mixing and using acrylics as well as their many different mediums, add-ins to change texture and consistency.

If you wish to share interesting discoveries or experiences feel free to email me at: squishart@gmail.com with Squish Art in the subject line.

DRYING AND STORING PAINTINGS

Keep picture faces and all painted surfaces from touching one another until completely dry. Do not put pictures away until they are completely dry. Small pictures dry to the touch in thirty to sixty minutes, but need overnight to cure completely (dry all the way through) in most cases. Drying can take several days in the case of very thick paint or large picture surfaces.

From the Liquitex website:

"Drying Time:
(http://www.liquitex.com/Products/products.cfm)
The dry time for all water based artists acrylic media depends on how quickly the water can evaporate from the application. This is dependent on:

- *The thickness of the product. For example, fluid varnishes will dry much more quickly than thick gels.*
- *The thickness of the application. For example, thin applications will dry much more quickly than thick applications.*
- *Relative temperature and humidity of the environment. For example, applications on warm, dry days will dry much faster than on cold, damp days.*
- *Absorbency of the substrate. For example, applications on absorbent surfaces will dry more quickly than on a hard, non-absorbent surface.*

There is a difference between dry time and cure time.
Dry time is when the surface feels dry to the touch.
Cure time is when the acrylic film is fully stable, close to its maximum durability, water resistant and less vulnerable to attack by mild solvents. This usually takes at least three days for thin applications and may take much longer (up to two weeks or more) for thick applications such as with Liquitex Super Heavy Body Color."

They also recommend speeding up drying time by using a hair dryer. I have not yet tried this and would recommend being very careful in the application of excess heat since paper is flammable.

If pictures do get stuck together you can usually separate them with as little tearing as possible by using a palette knife or thin spatula, sliding it between the pictures and applying a gentle, slow and steady pressure to "cut" them apart. Even with care and practice papers stuck firmly together or pressed together when wet can be ruined so take care to keep them separated for as long as possible, until fully cured is best.

To remove paper stuck on dry paint (it happens, especially if the weather is very hot or papers get pushed together) use a wet cloth or wet paper towel to soak only the unwanted paper bits. Carefully peel away the unwanted paper from the paint surface. Then use a soft cloth to gently polish your paint back to its normal luster. A very small amount of water may help the polishing process. If pieces are damaged beyond usefulness or your personal tolerance you can cut them up and use them to create a collage or five. Let your imagination, not your despair, run wild.

Save all pictures for later reappraisal and/or display. Artist's portfolios made of paper or cardboard are fairly cheap and keep pictures clean, corralled and reasonably flat. Artist Portfolios are also available in many other materials including plastic, aluminum, nylon and leather; they are accordingly priced by size as well as material ranging from a few dollars to several hundred. For storage I mostly use paper portfolios, such as Red Fiber Art Portfolios with plastic loop handles ranging in retail price from about $2.50 to $13.00. These expand to about 2 inches to hold quite a few paper pictures.

For storage only, I am undecided whether there is any real advantage to the ones with handles or those without handles except that if you have several to move at a time the handles seem to help. For handling in transportation I find it much easier to have a handle, especially in the larger sizes.

You can often find sales or non-name brands for even less. I suggest you look for prices as you go rather than just buying a few dozen of each to start, but you know your method and budget best.

I also use a couple of heavy-duty nylon portfolios for transporting pictures as these are much sturdier and more durable, as well as being somewhat water resistant.

===============

Feature Presentation

> Ghosts walk through this picture
> Sometimes you can see them
> Out the corner of your mind
> If you don't look just right

Making Art Happen

How to Squish Art?

Squish Art stands alone as an art technique. But you may also use Squishing Art to lead into the study of photography or representational art.

Also, do not forget the story, or stories, each picture holds inside itself. Use idea pebbles that you create from the artworks to trigger a story or poem. See Idea Pebbles section.

Several basic techniques are all that are necessary to begin Squish Art. These fall under three categories: PLACEMENT, PRESS and PULL. I have also developed others. Feel free to make up your own as well. But first we need some details:

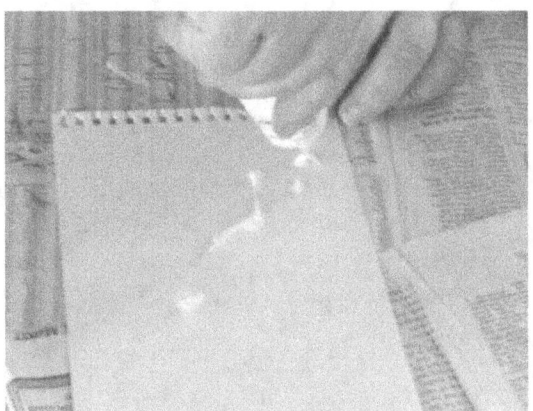

PLACEMENT of Paint on the paper and the choice/variety of colors forms the basis for each picture.

TECHNIQUE: Use paint directly from the tube and press paint out like expensive toothpaste or fancy cake-frosting. REMEMBER that you are going to be squishing this paint between pieces of paper so use paint sparingly at first, rather than excessively. It may take a try or three to find the amount that works for you.

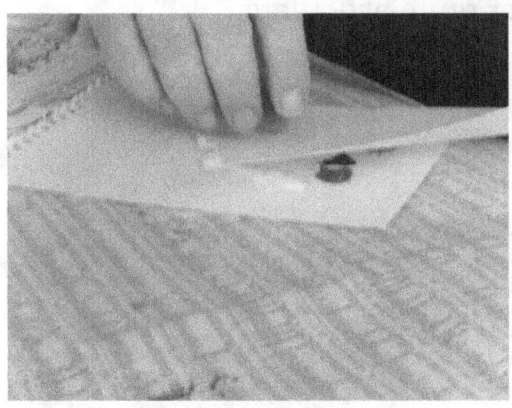

PRESS primarily determines spreading and mixing of the different color dots and bars. The harder you press down the more the paint spreads and mixes. Hardest is not always best here. I usually prefer a light to medium touch. It will take a few tries to get the optimum pressure for your taste or application.

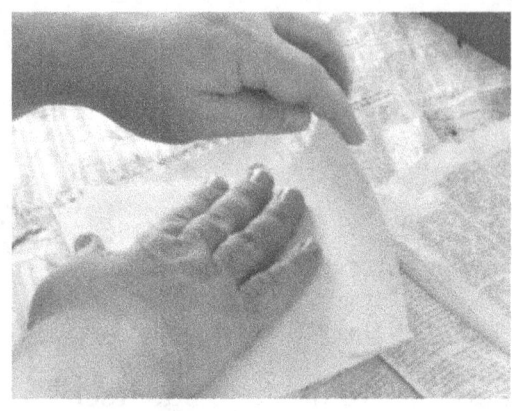 PULL primarily determines the directional flow of the picture. The speed of the pull changes texture and mix of the picture.

Practice pictures with different pulling techniques as well as different pressures.

================

Time Presses

Watches that don't care
What time it might be

People that buy them anyway
For
Reasons they can never quite articulate

Pulling The Picture — Overview

Place paint on your bottom piece of paper using Dots or Bars. Place a clean blank piece of paper on top of this dotted/barred sheet. This sheet will also be a picture. Let it. It is often more than a mirror image of the bottom. In the beginning, especially for younger children, this is a two-person operation. As hands and coordination mature it is possible to use an artist's clipboard to hold the bottom sheet for larger works. I now find it fairly easy to do even rather large pieces myself. I still enjoy and recommend working together whenever possible.

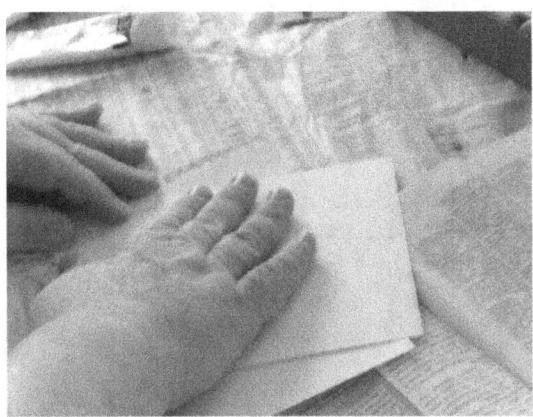 Press lightly (see PRESS BASICS) down on the top sheet while gently pulling the top sheet across the bottom (see PULL BASICS). This Squishing turns dots and/or bars of paint into a picture. The manner of pressing and pulling as well as speed and direction determine results.

With a bit of practice it is possible to anticipate results and design your bottom picture and even the top. {excellent image-ination practice!} Always use quality art paper for Squish Art.

Cheap paper not only tears easily, it wrinkles and will not hold its shape. 70lb, or heavier, acid free artist's paper (drawing or watercolor) seems to work fine. Size of the paper depends on the individual. Larger size paper should usually be somewhat heavier. Try colored art papers for variety.

DO NOT FORGET to lay down newspaper
or other guard (waste) sheets
to protect tables, sidewalks or floors.

Basic Placements

DOTS — Use small to medium sized dots of paint. I use dots about half the size of a Hershey's Chocolate Chip for average. A Hershey's Chocolate Kiss is very large, usually much too large, for a dot of paint in a 6x9 paper.

Place dots of different colors next to one another. This allows for lots of mixing of color at Squish Time. For concentration of a single color place several dots of matching color near one another.

BARS — Use a line of paint of varying thickness. It doesn't need to be straight. Feel free to swish or swoop. Lay a line of one color paint along, after or before another. Or lay it across at an angle. Different juxtapositions of color bars allow different top and bottom layers of color, different middle mixtures.

Before would mean ahead in the pulling direction, after behind in that direction. After bars will appear as the topmost color layer, before as underlayers.

It is good art technique to avoid contaminating in-tube color with other colors. While we want mixing on the page, it is considered good technique to avoid mixing another color inside or on the tube itself so that the color remains pristine for future use.

With a little practice it becomes easy to dot or bar without touching the paint tube to the paper or to other colors. If you get a bit in the wrong place wipe it off immediately (use damp paper towel); no harm done; no problem.

Dots & Bars Example

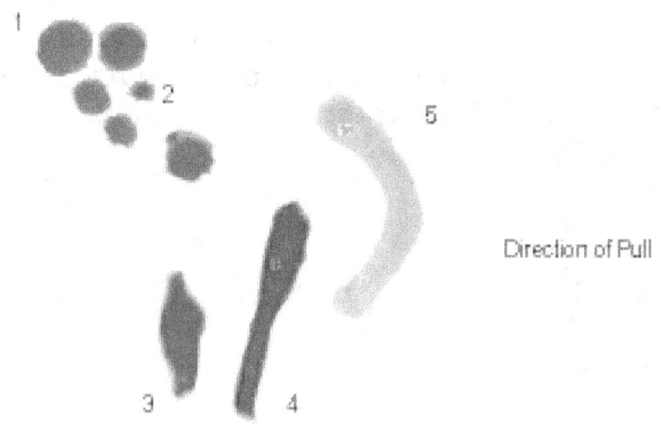

Direction of Pull

1 Large Blue dot {actual size approximately ½ inch}
2 Small Magenta dot {actual size approximately 1/8 inch}
3 Short stubby Red bar
4 Longish bar {actual size approximately 2½ inch}
5 Curved Tan bar

Note: I know these dots and bars are in black and white, but I left the color references in to help, one hopes, with your mental imaging.

Tan bar (5) is after the green bar (4). Red (3) is before both. Green will appear on top of tan after squishing. Red (3) will be on top of both. But there will be show through of each if colors are used sparingly.

Blue dots (1) will be on top of magenta dots (2). Both should partially cover tan bar (5).

An angled or turning pull will mix colors up even more.

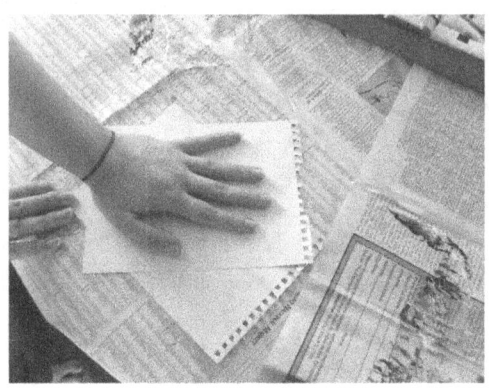

HARD — gives a very flat, quite spread out color dispersion. Too hard often yields a rather jumbled look.

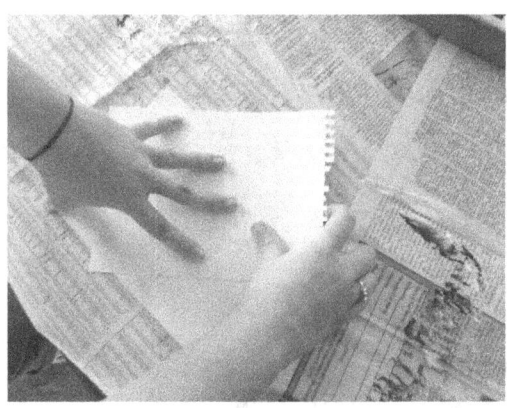

SOFT — Yields a more textured mix. Too soft a pressure will not mix the dots and bars enough to create something beyond themselves.

Pull Basics

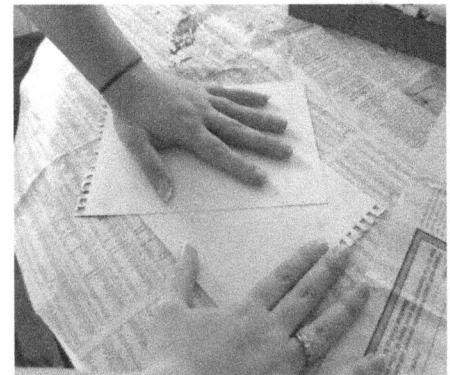

Start Pull

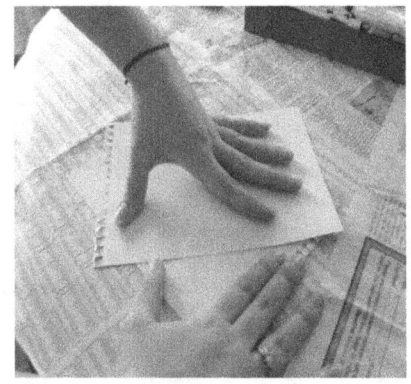

Push and Pull

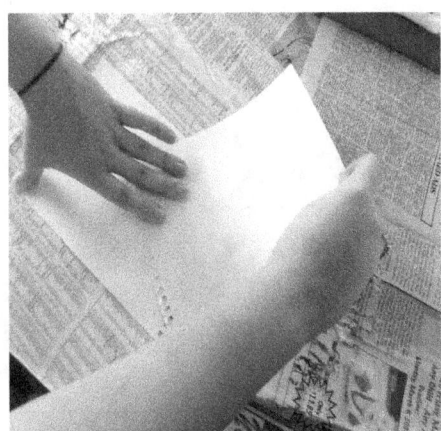

Lift top sheet to finish

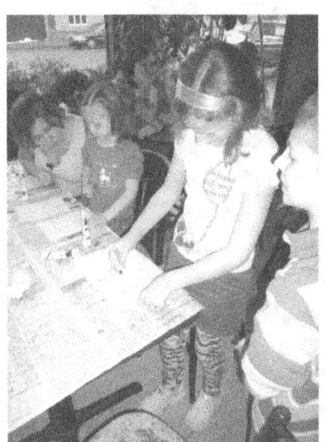

Concentration?

STRAIGHT — will give a fairly static look to a picture with all motion going left/right or up-down.

TURN — A gradual turn left or right while pulling will give a nice sweeping motion to the pieces. {Some folks have had success with turning a complete circle or close to one with little or no straight pull. See Severe Turn}

COMBINE TECHNIQUES to create eye-xciting pictures.

Painted Echoes

My mind keeps hearing this picture
On its coffee breaks and vacations

In empty elevators
This painting scrawls the walls

Every second echo
Instant-replays everything this painting ever said

Bigger Picture

Dogs play just to the left
Of all you can see out in this picture window.

Cats lick themselves right
And imagine butterflies so large
They cannot fit in this frame.

Intermediate Presses

LIFT — change the pressure at different points during the pull to create lofted textures. This works better with just a bit more paint. Be careful to inform pulling partner of large changes in pressure to avoid sudden loss of balance in either picture or partner.

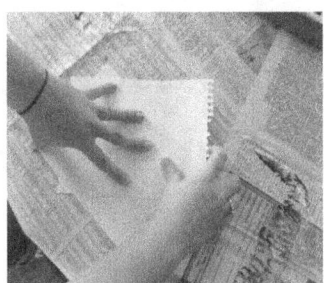

Spread Fingers

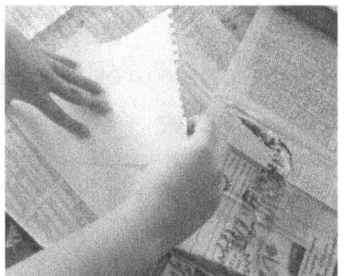

Lift while pulling

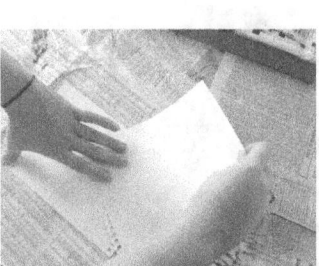

Finish Lift and pull

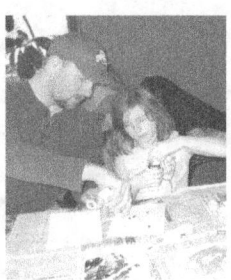

Who's Having More Fun?

TWISTing the pressure hand alters orientation of top page to bottom while the paper is being pulled -- yields interesting results, as does giving a major turn.

I often stop the pull momentarily during a twist, but do not release hold with pulling hand which would allow the papers to touch completely. See SEVERE TURN.

VARYING PRESSURE throughout the pull can produce varying textures and mixes. Experiment to find your favorites. Severe or unexpected changes can lead to torn paper. Don't be afraid to learn from your experiences.

PRESSING WITH FINGERTIPS only is an interesting pressure variation. Place the fingertips wide apart or vary their placement. Try using only two or three fingers. Did I already say, "Experiment?"

Intermediate Pulls

MULTIPLE TURNS — A gradual turn left and then right while pulling will give a nice side to side sweeping motion to the pieces. A small piece of paper may not allow room for many multiple turns.

SEVERE TURN — Circular pulling of top piece or opposite pulling of top and bottom pieces may produce startling color mixes and textures.

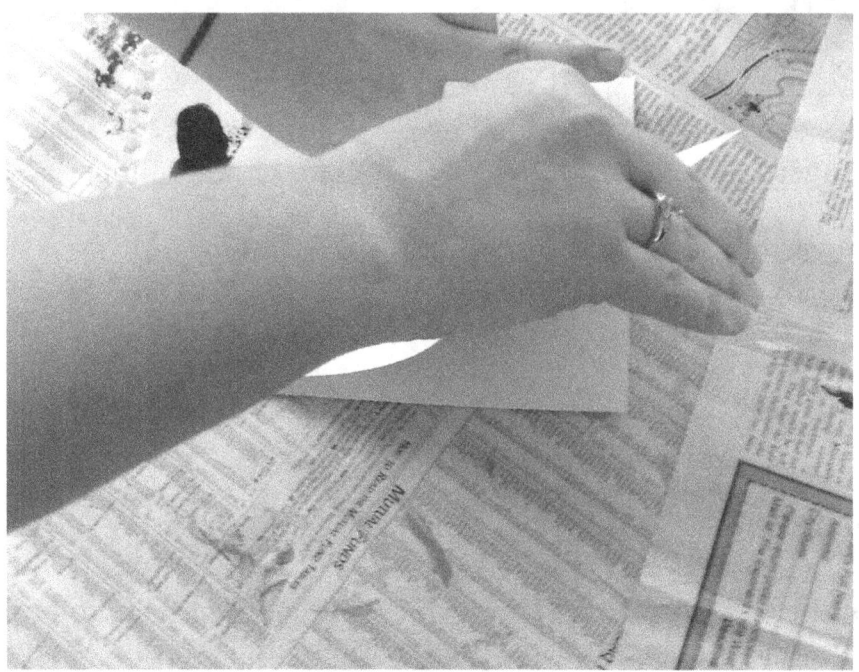

Pull and Turn

Alternative Techniques

More/Advanced Techniques

After an initial squishing:

Unmask layers of color. Remember that there are paint colors under the colors you see, especially if you have used a lot of paint. Reveal the layers using a palette knife or a small spatula (yes, the kitchen utensil) to dig or scratch for color. Create swirls or other patterns in the paint.

Squish or swirl texture, form or anything you can imagine into the painting. Use sponges; cut them into various shapes or shapelessness and swirl pat or swipe. Use a popsicle stick; whittle notches into the end or side and use it to move paint into textures and patterns you can love. Most art supply stores sell a relatively inexpensive set of wooden tools for shaping clay. These make interesting patterns for variety and experiment.

Squish Shapes, cut a sponge into an interesting shape and use it to squish colors below or above other shapes.

Hands, fingers, toes and elbows are all interesting textures or implements and they are all washable.

Some or all of these techniques can also be used without using a top paper to make the initial squish.

Feel free to combine Squish techniques with traditional and nontraditional art techniques. If you find any good ones write to me describing them.

One technique favored by some in my creativity workshops
is to simply fold the paper over onto the paint and press to get fairly symmetrical designs.
Try your own combinations!

Squishing Alternative Tools

I have found it interesting and useful to use a palette knife to spread large areas of paint, especially on larger papers. This gives you a much smaller sweep with each squish, but allows more control compared with using paper to squish. I have applied Squish Art techniques to the palette knife in much the same way as I used them with a top paper.

Sometimes you may wish to add to or subtract color (paint) from a squished picture. A painting knife (also called palette knife) is a useful tool and costs two to six dollars online depending primarily on size of blade and handle. Prices will vary at your local art store.

FYI: Although most folks use the term palette knife to refer to both styles there is a basic difference in the two. The palette knife is designed to be used to mix paints on the artist's palette and has a relatively shallow bend in shaft. The painting knife has a sharper bend to allow you to keep your knuckles out of the paint. I have found that either one can work for either purpose if you are careful.

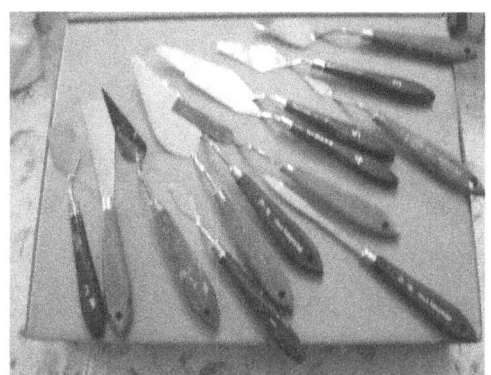

I have collected about a dozen and a half different sizes and shapes of these knives over the last decade or so. I also have tried and found useful at different times for varied effects various kitchen scrapers, spatulas and clay shaping tools as well as carving out my own wooden or cardboard scrapers. Sometimes I use sponges either whole or cut to shapes. Anything to get a texture going.

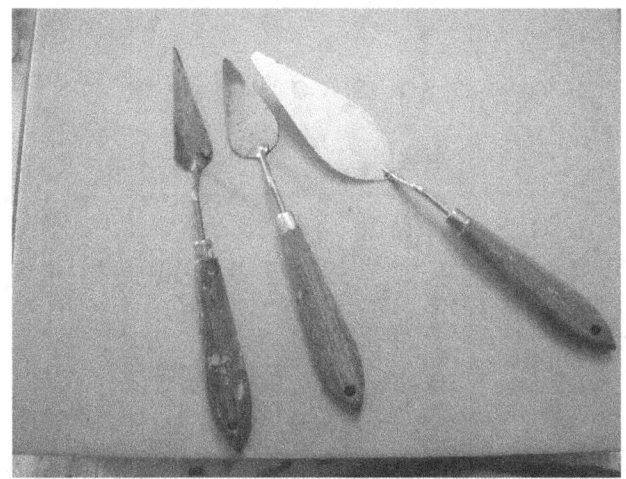 I find that I mostly reach first for the teardrop shaped knife in three sizes (left), both for spreading and whacking. Smaller or sharper edged knives can be used effectively for slicing. I prefer the "feel" of the unvarnished handles and find that the larger handles fit my hand better. The flex of the blade varies quite a bit as well. Try one or two and see how and what you like.

Quality can vary widely so look around a bit to see what you might like and can use most effectively. I found quite a selection of Liquitex brand painting knives at http://www.dickblick.com/products/liquitex-painting-knives/#photos. But I picked mine up one or two at a time over a decade in various art stores. Many colleges and universities have great art sections in their book stores.

I often use these knives or scrapers to squish the paints rather than a top sheet of paper nowadays, especially on larger works using more expensive papers, as I feel it gives more control. Please feel free to mix techniques to find ones you like. Continue to experiment. That is a large part of creativity, not to mention the joys of discovery.

I have tried a couple of cheap plastic palette knives for squishing, but I cannot recommend them. I didn't care for the feel of them, both in the hand and in contact with the paper. Also, I broke one of them on a hard scrape and gave myself a gouge and a handful of paint to boot, not to mention significantly altering my basic plan for the piece. It was a fun challenge fixing it though, the art, not the gouge. Please feel free to try out several options and decide for yourself what will work best for you.

Always clean knives and scrapers with dish soap and warm water as soon as you finish. Dry with a paper towel. This keeps the surfaces clean and free of paint buildup. Like any surface it is much easier to remove wet paint from the knives than to scrape the paint off after it has cured.

Whacking, slicing or scraping your squished picture

What is whacking? My basic whacking technique is to take a palette knife and use it like a hammer with the edge of the knife cutting into the paint and revealing layers below. I must admit I developed this in a snit over a squish that did not come anywhere near to my original design. All the colors I had planned and plopped had been submerged below a layer of bright red.

In frustration, I whacked the red blob with the edge of my handy palette knife. To my surprise this revealed those lost layers in its little knife-slice through the angry red. In addition the wet paint sort of bunched up around the wound providing 3-D textures. Delighted, I whacked again, harder, faster, slower. I noticed that the knife also picked up paint and transported it to other whacks. This provided both continuity and variety in the piece. It has since become one of my favorite pieces, *Notes From The Belly Of An Unsaved Whale.*

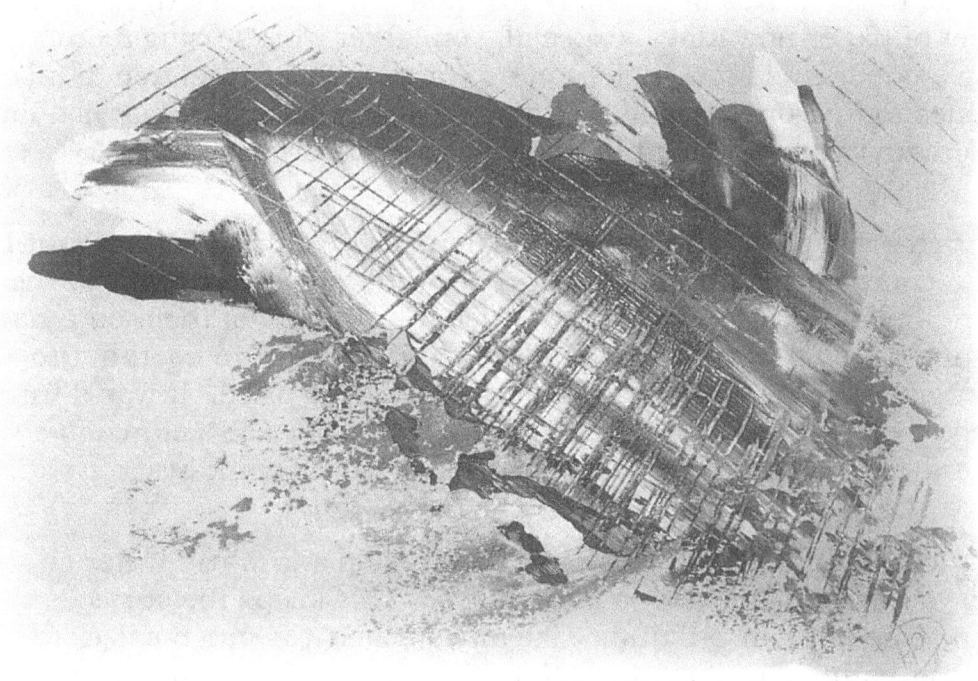

I think you can see the vigor and motion-emotion even better in black and white than in color although I still prefer the overall effect of the color version.

What is Scraping? I soon discovered or uncovered that a similar reveal could be accomplished by scraping away sections of too concentrated color to reveal whirlpools of colors below. That is when I discovered the plastic dough knife as a useful scraping tool for paint.

What is Slicing? The two aforementioned techniques led me to a combination that is often interesting as well. I usually use one or more of the palette knife blades to make smaller scrapes in multiple strokes to create patterns. Twisting and angling the blade in relation to the paper can create many organic effects which have aspects of both whacking and slicing.

Once again, let me say, feel free. Free your paints to mix. Let your techniques run amok and see what happens. Don't be disappointed if your first attempts are less than you hoped for. Like so many things in life and art the trick, to me, seems to be deciding when to stop and that comes with time and practice.

Names

Naming Your Picture

Pictures carry stories. Images can evoke ideas. Or maybe your imagination carries stories which the pictures evoke. Sometimes a picture might have a special song inside it. Or it brings out a song in you. Let it sing.

Look at a picture you have created. What is happening; what story do you see? What images do you see? Where did the image(s) come from? Where are they going? Are there novels in there? Short stories?

Can you give the picture a name? Say it out loud and see if it fits. Turn the picture upside down and all around; view it from any and all directions to see what might be hidden therein. Does its name change when the view changes? Is one picture direction better than another? Is there a best way? One you like best? One that really says something to you? I find, for most pieces, that one name-idea intersection has a tendency to dominate and supercede all others. I have a few works that ended up with two or more names, but not many.

Eventually I realized that, even though only one idea-name fit best with a particular picture those other idea intersections were also worth saving. Thus began the idea pebbles collections (see more of pebbles in the next section) which led to an entirely different creative tool.

Suggestions For Seeing Art

The art of seeing is essential to creativity. For most of us this means using not just the eyes in their regular functions, but going beyond. Yogi Berra is often quoted as saying "Sometimes you can observe a lot just by looking."

How many times do you look, but not really see, not take in and process everything around you. For most of us that is most of the time. We all have our editors built up to help us process only what we need to deal with at any one time. Or we impose previous versions of a scene over the actual one just because it is easier than taking time to see something new.

One example of this was brought home to me many years ago. My wife and I purchased our house from my parents when they moved on. I had lived in that house for several years before that. When we built the house I had picked the colors for my bedroom: federal blue carpet, matching blue walls, and a blue-white ceiling with cream woodwork. My family called it "The Blue Room." I thought that a great name for the den of the brooding teenaged boy which I was then.

When we moved in a decade or so later we took the master bedroom and used The Blue Room as a spare bedroom. When we first got an Apple II computer The Blue Room seemed an ideal place to house the computer and all its paraphernalia.

Finally, the realization. A friend of ours who shared our interest in computers, among other things, was over one evening and asked to see our computer setup. I was happy to have him see it, but occupied with something else immediately so I gave him the simple directions: "Top of the stairs, The Blue Room on the left." He came back down after a few moments and asked if I meant the room with the bright orange walls that had the computer in it. I was both surprised and startled to find when we trekked back up the stairs that, indeed, the walls were a hideous, to my eye, shade of orange, not blue at all. We had been living in that house for more than two years. I had been working in that room for more than six months on the computer and had never processed the simple visual fact that someone, my father no doubt, had painted the walls such radically different color. My personal filter had simply blocked that major difference out.

This incident caused me to become aware, over time, of other instances of the same thing: a remembered landmark long gone, an old friend aging, was that car always that shade of green. I also became aware that most people do this all the time without noticing.

This is one thing that Squish Art can help you move out of. You need to use fresh eyes to look at a Squish Art piece and get the maximum effect. If you don't see anything on first glance close your eyes and open new ones. Let your filters slip and your editor sleep. Let your ideas flow and grow.

Open your mind. This is, or can be, a scary thing when first encountered. The Squish Art process is a good and controlled way to get started. Warning! Don't throw out your filters and editor completely. They are there to help you manage everyday life by concentrating on those things that are important or that stand out for some reason. DO become aware of their existence and cultivate the ability to override them when it makes sense.

As far as seeing to create idea pebbles it is important to let ideas flow without filtering, editing or censorship. Get them out and write them down. You can evaluate and edit later as needed. Build on ideas others toss out as well as on your own.

Picture Stories and Picture Poems

What did the people or creatures do to get to where they are in this picture? Why are they there? Where are they going? If they were writing letters to a friend after they got home, what would they say? Ask who, what, when, where, why and why not.

Use the answers to tell a story. Write a poem to describe the feelings you get from viewing this picture. Write a poem about waiting for the stories to come.

Just stop a moment or three and let the picture move your mind. Close your eyes and imagine what the picture thinks about when you go to bed. What are its aspirations, its plans for future and family and fame?

==================

Catch

Took three days off from writing
Things down.
I'm always writing things up
In my head.
At least I seem to me to be.

That means
At least six catch-up poems
Are required.

Unfortunately,
I have sixty waiting in line.
All of them seem to have valid tickets.

Different Names For Different Sames

Share the picture with a friend and ask them to name and story or poem the picture. No two people view any picture exactly the same way, but there are often similarities within a group.

I have found that there are some Squish pictures wherein almost everyone sees the same thing, hair, windmills, fish or a face or a dog or a footprint. There are other pictures where six people see sixteen different things. Some of my favorite ones are where I see six different pictures, all with their own names and stories.

Compare stories, names or poems. Talk about how and why your story, poem, picture title is different. Keep lists of titles you didn't use for this picture. Those ideas might be worth a poem or story as well. Discuss what made you choose the way you did. Point out what you saw. Relax and try to see what others saw.

You have discovered art. You have exercised your imagination. I hope you continue to have as much fun with it as I do.

After you've spent some time with basic Squish techniques feel free to move on to more advanced ones that follow. Make up your own. Send me some of your best ideas. I'll try to share some of them in the next edition.

=================

Dreamwork

T'other night I . . .
I dreamed I was a painting
Just like this one
Only taller, with lots more blue.

Writing The Story

Remember that stories live everywhere not just in abstract pictures.

Every picture tells a story. Some tell many stories. Does every story tell a picture? Think up a story and Squish pictures to go with it. Plan a Squish picture and see how close the final outcome is to your initial idea.

Keep experimenting. Keep thinking.
Keep art in your life and life in your art.

Squish Art Experience Summary

Moving freely
From "What is this picture?"
To "What do you see in there?"
To "What in the world are they doing in here?"

To "What/Who are these people-things in this picture?"
To "Where are they going?
Then "Where have they been?"
Finally (or not) "Why did they come here?"

Idea Pebbles

Idea Pebbles Introduction

Many people find it a lot of work to get started with anything creative. Or maybe it is hard to come up with a NEW idea. How can you tell if an idea is completely new? If it is brand new, if no one has ever even thought of it before what can you do with it? Often we find ourselves dealing with, or avoiding dealing with, these and similar questions and never getting around to doing any creating.

In creating my own poems I found that I would run out of ideas and have to stop writing for lack of material rather than lack of time or energy. I found this frustrating as have most of the writers and artists I have discussed this problem with. They even have composed cute names for it: Writer's Block, Lack of inspiration, The Stares, Blank Page Rage and probably hundreds of others; you may have your own. This is where Idea Pebbles, Pebbles for short, come into play.

What about all those extra names?

At first I only used the finished and named Squish Art to generate poems, usually only one poem per picture. After several months, however, it came clear to me that the ideas/name options that we didn't use to attach to a picture might be as valid poem fodder as those we did use. Shortly thereafter I came up with the name Idea Pebbles. I began saving those names, phrases, ideas as well and began compiling a list in a Word document. A year or so later I had so many that it was hard to pick out one or two to use for any given poem so I created a computer program to generate random pebble groupings such as those given in the Appendix A.

Who-What-Why are Pebbles

Pebbles are phrases or ideas captured and collected for later use in whatever creative activity you may care to use them.

Saving these pebbles separates the creative process into several stages so that you do not need to come up with ideas and applications thereof in the same space-time intersections.

I developed the pebbles process/concept in order to help me create poems at any time, not only when "The Mood" strikes me.

The original pebbles concept and metaphor was to imagine my self as a quiet pond with no ideas or thoughts at all (a common meditation technique). The idea pebble is then dropped, tossed or skipped into or across the pond, your mind. As the ripples grow out from the pebbles passage they become the poem or develop into your story ideas.

I still find it comforting to return to that basic idealization some times. Even though, after a decade and a half of using idea pebbles the ripplings come fairly quickly most of the time. That is, the mind, once opened is more easily opened again.

Creating and Storing Pebbles

For many folks the creation portion of the process, getting the pebbles to create themselves, is a difficult task. I find that newcomers to the workshops are often reluctant to let down their filters and other internal barriers and simply let their ideas flow.

Like many other activities then it is often useful to have a guide to help you over that beginning hurdle. Usually, the ideas flow fairly freely once the participants feel safe and free to let their internal ideas loose. I saw a book in the bookstore one time titled, "Let Your Crazy Person Sing." Inner Child, Crazy Person, Freedom, wherever you are hiding them ideas are lurking in there. Where do new ideas come from? You need to let your internal, or crazy, person loose.

Think of your newly created art as a color Rorschach blot. What do you see? What does it bring to mind. Yes, these are often sexual or asocial thoughts; go with it.

Although I can now, after years of practice, generate several pages of pebbles on my own I still find it interesting and pleasant to work with others in a group settings to bring out amalgamations of ideas. In most case this generates idea pebbles that no single participant would have come up with on their own. Perhaps we could call this a form of group sanity.

General Guidelines For Use of Poem Pebbles

Use the Random Pebble Groups I have provided for you in the Appendix A or those you have generated. Take a Pebble or four. Put them side-by-side to create a new idea. Use that to juxtapositioning to start a story or poem.

Through practice we have decided that three Pebbles at a time works well. This gives enough diversity of challenge to require some creative movement off-center, but not so bizarre-much as to cause total brain malfunction.

Try selecting a group of 5 from the random list. Give it to someone else. Tell them to pick any 3 of those 5 and use them to generate a poem or story. Ask them to pick one for your use.

Do not be limited by these Pebbles. Feel free to modify the Pebbles to suit your poem needs. For exercise try to play them as they lie, for they do lie the sneaky little worms; they lie in your mind whispering and gossiping about us and . . .

Get it out of your head in a poem on paper off your mind.

Individual poets and others have developed there own ways to use these pebbles in addition to the one given in the guidelines above. Here are a few they have shared with me:

Grab Bag 1: cut the printed pebbles apart into individual pebbles. Work on a Xerox or printed copy to save the book for reuse. Put all the slips into a special bag created for this purpose. Or use an old purse. Fit your own fits here. It is your bag.

Without peeking, you are allowed to wish if you must, pick one or three out of the bag. Use these as you like or according to the guidelines above.

Grab Bag 2: same as Grab Bag 1 except cut your pebbles into the groups as given.

Dictonary Mystery Tour: take the printed pages intact. Close your eyes and move a pencil over the page putting it gently down to select a Pebble group. Flip pages or have a friend flip a page or so to help further randomize the selections. Make sure to wait before the pencil plunging part so your friend has her or his hand out of the road of your plunging pencil point. Ouch!

This one is named from the dictionary game where one person opens the dictionary (It's a big book!) to a random page and places a finger blindly down on a word. The other players then write a definition of the chosen word. They all then vote on which of their definitions is best. The winner is of that round is the player who gets the most votes.

Preserving
And Appreciating
Your Art

Archiving and Displaying

Very flat pictures may be mounted in ready-made photo frames. Most of your Squish Art pictures will probably require matting to protect the texture. Commercial mattes for photos work well and can be found on sale at many department and discount stores. Larger sizes become more expensive. Custom matting and framing is available, but typically expensive.

I usually do my own matting. The techniques involved are not that difficult. The major expense is the angle-cutting apparatus that gives you that professional reveal to surround your work. I use a logan-301s-compact-mat-cutter. I got it on a clearance sale a number of years ago. I found it recently on the DickBlick (See Bibliography) site for about $70 plus shipping. Retail price was listed there at about $120.

Before I found this I used the Dexter matte cutter (listed online for about $22) which is just a handheld Xacto knife blade holder which needs a straight edge to run against. I made my own press and straight edge mechanism out of plywood, brass hinges and aluminum bar. It was large and unwieldy, but worked well overall after I got used to it. The compact version is easy to use and transport, but I occasionally find it takes work to make it fit some size cuts.

You can buy matte board in many colors and sizes. I usually buy larger sizes, about 2.5 by 3.5 feet, and cut them down as needed. Also, the center piece you cut out to show a large work can be used to matte one or more smaller works. Prices vary greatly depending on size and type of matte board. Online prices at one site for the 32" by 40" size board ran from $12 to $40 each. I suggest you start with the less expensive boards and see how you like the look. The cheaper "Decorative" style is usually allows the widest choice of colors. Again, make sure the materials are acid-free, also labeled archival.

Painted plywood or hardboard makes a nice display background for your pictures and is relatively cheap. Photo background paper also works well. It is available in rolls or sheets in many different colors and even patterns. Wait! Is this someplace we can put our imaginations to work once more. Could be?

Resist the temptation to pin or tape pictures up. This temptation is especially strong if you use corkboard or similar soft material. Pins, nails, etc. put permanent holes in the paper. Most tapes do not come off cleanly, but rip parts of the paper off with them. For short term mounting I find that a poster adhesive such as PosterTAK from SuperGlue or Scotch 109 Removable (Mounting) Poster Tape from 3M works well.

The professional way to mount your paper works on matte board is to use art hinges; many sources suggest using them at the top of the work only to allow it to float behind the matte board. You can make your own hinges from Japanese rice paper or use a commercial type. Make sure that you or your framer use archival, acid-free materials to preserve your works.

For more information on mounting take a browse through your local library or bookstore or online. Try "paper art hinges" and "mounting paper art," "Matte board" (also Mat board or matting board) or "framing" as a beginning search key.

Appendices

Appendix A – Sample Pebbles

Pebble Samples in Random Pebble Groupings

These individual Pebbles were created and compiled at our dining room table and at many creativity workshops and are provided for your use in creating your own poems, stories, titles or melt-ups.

Once they have been recorded I type them into a text file and save them on disk. I have written a Visual Basic computer program which I named *Strange Universes* to randomly create these pebble groups from any text file. Using this or a similar computer program you can create your own Pebble files if you prefer or add to the ones I provide with the program (holding over 3,300 Idea Pebbles at last count); program and Pebbles text file currently packaged separately from this book.

I have provided here a list of 200 groups of five random pebbles each to get you started. These all came from the same Pebbles file and therefore there may be some overlap of individual Pebbles in the different groups. They were generated using the *Strange Universes* computer program.

1

Tossing something dirty
Melted rainbow arc
Chase the carrousel
Footprints of the lobster blues
Under heel

2
Rich with the blues
Disgust Discussed Digest & the DDD
        rating system
Fisher kink
On the verge of merry
Pubescent, tumescent, Iridescent
        adolescent angst

3
Cement pond
First great idea of the day
Used tie
Positively peculiar dying fall
Fisher kink

4
Headless man walking with big yellow
        shoes
Challenger ethos
Toucan
Vulture four-play
Inferno inside

5
Echoes of a pixie
Sideways elephant nodding yes
Carpenter's circular saw
Dumb blonde fertility goddess
Blood on my shoe

6
Dark giant cupped hand
Stomping the blood pool
Love his pants
Yellow bells all around
Chomping at the Yosemite

7

Ice skater carrying baton
Caterpillar golfer
Syntaxual shower
Stunt tears on panda bear
World pottery firing

8
Women who burn you with their glance
Red phoenix in a blue crystal cage
Cat turning
Two Chinese princesses
Rocket surfing the ocean

9
Teeter-totter
What the saxophone said
Purple passion under the weeping
        willow
Morning waterfalls
Dysfunctional parroting

10
Udder socks
Multicolored centipede rolled up
Little brother is on spin dry
Tippy's nightmares
Universe with everything on it in a face

11
Smiling worms
Priest backpack
Footprints in blue
What do the stones say?
Horse over the rainbow

12
Cabbage slaw serenade
Green pepper bird?s brain
Tree swingers
Dragon trippin'
Reason for no air conditioning

13
Two-facing the music
Scene from a turkey
Flight of the Dodo
I see a red rat
Decapitated lizard

14
Abstract fruit basket
Lemur under burning bush
Brain exploding
Psychedelic snail that threw barbells in
    the air
Fowl mood

15
Robot penguin
Alas poor Yorick
Women with dogs
Dancers whirl, Coyote watches
Patchwork clothesline

16
Flame
Blue fog with pink frog
Nightmares having nightmares
Zookeeper teasing blue hippo
Clowns smile even when sad

17
Prismatic peacock
Exploding trees
Pink froggy
Blue cat
Haley's comet inverted

18
Sperm whale
Sunken sun
Tossing your jalapenos
Green pepper bird's brain
The shining mermaids

19
On the eighth day it all went to shit
Stuck in your teats
Transvestite John, the Baptist
Curled up lying dragons
Stunt tears on panda bear

20
Brainiac attack with word people
Peacock with tail folded
Designed to capture
Forced abortion
Drugs running down the neck of a
    bottle

21
Hippo zookeeper
Isadora dunkin' donuts
The dog and the hare
Melting in a jazz shire
Crescent pond

22
Slain buffalo saving a buffalo
Purple pinkie
Buddhist magicians
Flash Gordon's ship
Blue gondolier

23
Bear water-skiing
Stuck in your teats
Tropical revolution
Blue ice skates with pixie hat
Back when rabbits laid eggs

24
Palm Sunday Island
Blue escargot
Don King with flames
Bad day at the fair
I want out

25
Cosmic turd with iridescent turd
Past the speed
Saving slain buffalo
Storm in a gin bottle
She's laying down, she's laying down

26
Two pencils kissing
Bruisin' souls
Some kind of confusion
Heave-hoes
Little brother is on spin dry
27
Rodeo over the mountain
The scream in San Francisco
Dog sitting on telephone
Seggsual
Slain buffalo

28
Coyote canyon suite
Is Benedictine green?
Bob and the Dradle-ettes
Tongue with nest on top
Pink raptor

29
Bubble gum explosion
Red chicken hand grenade
Monkey and the monkey's mind
Fabio's daily pheromone transfusion
Sufficient dragons

30
Spin doctor
Unsuccessful plastic surgery
Steamin' demon pasta
Coffin table
Crawdad swimming in a pool of blood
31
Aroma behind oranges
Glacial splash
Cousin It pumping iron
Two ducks playing soccer
Blood cliffs

32
Stop thinking -- I'm padless
Sensible retrospections
Banshee on a horse
Spider trap
Eye of the vortex

33
Pigeons in my eyes
Tree wings
RRCEWW
T rex in a Dodge truck
Goose with sunglasses

34
Cothera aftermath
Mosaic with shield
Cheshire cat forgot to grin
Floppy-ear dog
That's where the dragon took me

35
Caterpillar gone crazy
Woman morphing into lion
Gold crush
Hair magnet
Fifty shapes distincted into one purple
        blob

36
Lightning with purple clouds
Bird drumming as flies
Hot dog in a moldy bun
Yellow bat hanging
When the rainbow hit the fan

37
Worm eating tail
Fish chasing fish jumping
Oscar's wet dream
Crying mermaid with sea in her hair
Kissing your jalapenos

38
French street orphan looking into the
        sky
Pterodactyl
Freeze that finger
Psychedelic tempos
When life gives you lemmings

39
Japanese No mask
Horse explosion
Fingers and toes intertwined
Nerd attacking human
Abalone shell bologna
40
Depressing Christmas
Woman wit balloons
Scene from a carousel
Vulture beak WITH joker
Peeping boy

41
Depressed neck tie
Sky woman swallowed by the moon
Jelly fighter
Floorway
Behind a waterfall

42

Yellow attack rabbit
Stepping stone to Japanese pagoda
Normally naughty nights
Nest of elephants
Things dead birds eat

43
She pinked me
Figures with implants
Beaver Cleaver meets Emmett Kelly
Tao-n-out
Feeding the beast

44
Festival
Emperor goes wading
Lizard egg in jest
Fruity pebbles in a plane crash
Attack of the dark monster

45
Medusa's bad hair day
Dancing dolphins
Lion rowing a boat
Grape conga line
Grandma's swamp garden

46
Segment of an ant
Pterodactyl
Stardust format
Guy laying on back
Blue ferrets jumping rope

47
Love his socks
Flight of the penguin
Leopard doughnuts
Golden eagle swoosh
Sea creature

48
Diana's bow
The vision Quest ends at a foreign Shore
Dyslexic witches' cauldron
Chernobyl Christmas lights
Hunting season opens

49
Fruitfly's nightmare
Things dead birds eat
Slain buffalo saving a buffalo
Blue broken bucking bronco with kitty
Curendera's unconscious

50
Cars coming after the morning, they
            honk not
God and her stupid dog
Last time I got drunk
Duck-down pumps
Rebellious lemmings

51
What cannonballs think about . . .
Kissing goodbye to negative sandwich
God in blue leotard
Tumbleweed Christmas tree
Blue gar trying to catch a frog

52
And the land mine said
Dragon
Blue domino
When the butterfly crashes
Fifty shapes in one purple blob

53
Green kangaroo eating yellow Easter egg
Cowboys' dream
Head hidden behind blue explosion
Little brother is on spin dry
Birth of a betrayal

54
Hippo zookeeper
Swan rider pursued by dragons
Rabbit with computer backpack
Blues blender
Blue bird of happiness hits the
    windshield

55
Invisible man with green tie
Apes swinging through me?s
Frogman Olympian speed eater
Waiting for breakfast or something like
    her
Rainbow grackles

56
Push-ups are a hazard to health
It's a bitch to be a clown on Mondays!
Horse with a cow attached
Coat of many fishes
Dinosaur puke

57
Glory days
Coffee table with red rubbers
Medusa needs a manicure
Revenge of the piranha
Carpenter's circular saw

58
Barney got squished
White seal with blue background
Oriental orgasm in the rain
Elvis butterflies
Rudolph the red-nosed Easter rabbit

59
Wings of wax
Something cotton candy in her walk
Festive Great Wall of China
The craw of time
Banana curl sundae with green nuts

60
Charging up green hills
Isis-metrics
Doughnut hole in my soul
Anteater
Steamin' demon pasta

61
Fireworks fizzle
Red ladies dancing
Green conger
Coral snake biting purple hand
Dirty yards

62
Violin violence
Burning bush
Imagine this clown
Dance of the fans
Hot dog in a moldy bun

63
Monkey walking
The bride wore beige
Universe with everything on it in a face
Saxophone
What the floor sees when you dance

64
Dancing blue fairy
Purple pauvrocito
Revenge of the absurd
Genie Carson?s worst wife
Apes trying to compose

65
Inferno inside your chest
Date with Stardust Sally
Green fox hiding from red farmer
Green pepper bird's brain
Blurred riders on a green carousel

66
Race squids
Riding the whirlwind
Lizard just ate egg in nest
Transvestite John, the Baptist
Maneater with goat knees

67
Cypress fire
Creative mangling
Hammer and sickle
Gold rust gold rush
Unmasking of Mary
68
Quivering arrows
Spilled horn of plenty
Free-flying furious furies
Joan of triumph
Date with a nightmare moustache

69
Upwardly mobile pig
Man in the middle
Green pepper bird?s brain
This way out
Chinese dragon

70
Calm-bidextrous
Thinking of dolphins
Oh! Look at that duck.
Turkey Trotsky
Swatting between parrots

71
Leaping dolphin
Sky woman swallowed by the moon
Tussling slingshots
Zoo keeper teasing blue hippo
Frisbee frog & fearless dog rex

72
Blue woman, copper sea
Fear children learn in unkindergarten
Yellow cat smiling
Blue cat flame
Mouse & bird mating

73
Dancing paw print to paw print
Pegasus catcher
Montezuma with blues completes
        revenge
Rebellious lemmings
Cupid with conservatism

74
Fruit aroma over the blue kidney
I'm making out a face
Mermaid on Viking ship
Stupid people
Echo of dancing kittens

75
Hunchback swing dancers
First belly-flop of the summer
Dirt waffles
Carb lizards
Blues uprising

76
Wanda and Wendy Sue ate my heart
Tapdancing comet
Mad person
Depressing Christmas
Wine-stained lips

77
Submarine in a mind field
Brainstorms poem pebbles
Pastel tear droppings
Birth of woman
Attack of the elephant mice

78
Irish Kundalini
Fairy surfing the grapes
Happy hippo
Aroma over a bowl of oranges
Sunbeam's ribbon dance

79
Ghost of a dead blue pigeon
Squid world
Dragons
Two feet wide
A door into summer
80
Exodus from Camelot on a bicycle
White seal with blue background
Red yoga
Psychedelic tempos
Submarine carrying out an explosion

81
Red anteater blues
Fisher price is right
Sperm swimming to the penis
Peace dove in the nearest foxhole
Hairy mammoth

82
Clown in chaos
Man running from a meteor shower
Slender purple lady with acorn
Turkey Trotsky
Horse eating the greener grass

83
Eagle anchor
Spring champagne
Smeared blood
Bottle opener
Skull lechery

84
Blues uprising
Airscape
Lemming without a cause
Psychedelic cocktail party
Skiing Venice

85
Bear water-skiing
Barely beaten eggs
Loop doughnuts
Yellow belles
Upbeat blues

86
Pi eaters
Birds copulating
Floppy-ear dog
Cannonball
Submarine in a mind field

87
Wild iris polka
Cabbage slaw serenade
The swinging rope
Huddled before the wind
Egyptian women

88
Lady of the cosmos
Fisher fissure
Yoga class for squid
Purple pixie
Thinking of

89
Water life collage
Migration of the Bird Woman
Lizards over the moon
Pastel tear droppings
Michico rides a green dragon in the rain

90
My fingers are wise guys
Assonant allusion
Cave painting with deer
Cat disintegration
Two camels kissing

91
Enlarged view of artist's paintbrush
Kabuki dancer
Barney got squished
Two-year old's memory of the cemetery
Slimed again

92
Pretty lady with long hair
Sunset factory, lunch break
Squaring the abalone circle
Retired VW Beetle
Smear of blood on the morning after
        with yellow

93
Boopa Loopa
Coral snake
Penguin face down
Blue escargot
Indian fire goes out-rageous

94
Car skeleton
Water life collage
Fowl mood
T rex in a Dodge truck
Easter duck diarrhea

95
Something stuck in your teats
Alien teddy bears
Swimming with sharks
Square dance with snorkels
Surprising thistles

96
Lioness harvest
Melting in a jazz shire
Two camels kissing two pencils
Indians heretofore untouched
Fresh hot vanilla eclairs in my dreams

97
Out of water to see water
UFO
Cosmic birth
Dirty yards
Man running from a meteor shower

98
Lioness harvest
Blue heron stuck in mud
When good fireworks go bad
Puking dinosaurs
Pet murders through the backyard fence

99
Purple Pisces
Melted rainbow ark
Evolving ethos
Two pencils kissing
Sky woman swallowed by the moon

100
Shining teddy Bear
Vulture four-play
Huddled against the wind
Clean green fat hat lady
Heart of the indigo dream

101
Pig with glasses blond miss piggy
Read from behind
Fish climbing out of water
Tidal wives
Bruised bruisers

102
Echo of dancing kittens
Polar bear kicking in the mud
Dolphin fireworks
Blue dream of green frog
Dragons

103
Broken bananas
Used tie
French clown, English spelling
Gangs of dogs on bicycles
Chippendale

104
Crawdad swimming in a pool of blood
Zookeeper teasing blue hippo
Green cougar
Mouse on bird
What Tchaikovsky was looking at

105
Beaver Cleaver meets Emmett Kelly
Woman wit balloons
Rainbow laundry day
Crab with long tentacles
Palm Sunday Island

106
Dogs on bicycles
Sailing the copper sea
Violet violin
Back when rabbits laid eggs
Blond vulture's breakfast

107
Nautilus
Brainiac attack with word people
Seaweed cactus derangement
Bare-naked rainbows
Robot penguin

108
Up against the wall
Nine-G force most a human can take
Festive Great Wall of China
Bruised bruisers
Dog eating intensive boat

109
The red run
The cat is smiling . . . The dog is not
Thoughts we never share
Hammer and sickle
Lost turkey feathers

110
Shrimp on the Barbie Doll
Cosmic coffee ring
Whale trails
Shark going down
Montezuma with blue contemplates
        revenge

111
Shower of cosmic whores
Merry go round vomit
The swinging rope
Dangerous toothpaste
Gentleman juggling three green jugs

112
Pseudo-cannibal snoopy
Alas poor Yorick
Bumper clouds
Dying pumpkin
Tickles are free

113
Mother Earth meltdown
Scarab poop
Dali's red moustache
Alien hating frenzy
Really crazy chair
114
Addle-brained Abyssinian
Copper cotton candy kettle
Face with hair and pigtails
Portrayal of an oxyidiot
Dogs on bicycles

115
Peacock with tail folded
Ram
Drunk skunk in a squirrel whirl
Fire with glasses on
Blue mouse

116
Crooked horse shoes
Brain inc.
Egyptian women with dogs
Rat chasing fish
The shadow of my life

117
Bird taking final flying lesson
Some kind of dog fondling a cat
Confusion with exit sign
Kokapelli with fruitcake
Fish swimming in hat

118
Aurora's roller coach
Don't mess with my grits
Lounge lizard shirts
Rainbow rollercoaster
Bhudda's hand

119
UFO
It's a bitch to be a clown on
            Wednesdays!
Bear water-skiing
Dog sitting on telephone
Rainbow vulture

120
Buzzard in weird hat
Person swimming with sharks
The touch of the painter's hand
Rocket surfing the ocean
Lobster machineguns

121
Multicolored centipede rolled up
Toucan on the toilet
Ethos
Liars' lyre
Whale shark with pompadour
122
Birth of something
Eat me lovers who eat you first
Melting wind cones
Bumper whales
Cement pond

123
Midnight butterfly sunspots
Scratch me back
Ice sickles on a crazy man
Hippo heavens
Sunken sun

124
Sparrow
Meteor crashing against water
Seascape at 180 mph
Rainbows dripping from a dead hand
Promissory people

125
Silent supreme
Quick draw me down
Pelican naked woman
Old green eggs and hail
Found floating

126
Children sliding downhill from castle
Pineapple cuneiform
Apes swinging through trees
Pigeons in my eyes
Whimpering pink orgasms

127
Nerd attacking human
Don King with flames for hair
My hand is purple because I got bit
Confetti energy bars
Entrails in the sky

128
Colbaine on cocaine
Lambidextrose
Ram
Meteor flames
Dragons

129
Slender purple lady with corns
Running away from shadow puppets
Green kangaroo eating yellow Easter egg
Martian-Mallow
Lizards over the moon

130
Confusion with exit sign
Apocalypse in the fourth
Picasso's dead body
I like the swooshiness
Two diamond eyes

131
Now I see the face
Turtles trying to act like tadpoles
Collision of dog, schoolbus and
          interstellar comet
Big package under the Christmas tree
Skull season

132
Turtles trying to act like circus
          performers
Dream catcher
Red yoga
Challenger ethos
Sometimes I see a D O G

133
Hummingbird doing 'you don't wanna
          know'
Double-ought, single barrel
Two dogs and a psychedelic-painted
          turtle
Circulating distance
Negative fire

134
Evil-ution
Challenger ethos
Drag-on
Buffalo with scorpion's tail
Pink termite with bad attitude

135
Explosion at the candy factory
The slime salesperson
Cosmic turd with iridescent turd
Huddled against the wind
Turtles trying to act like tadpoles

136
Back when rabbits laid eggs
Electric eel chasing its tail
Blue platypus playing soccer
Blue footprints
Chinese acrobats with sock puppets

137
Caramel above
Abstractions addle the brain
Not totally decapitated
Sexier than new-mown baby lambs
God watches his destructive sources

138
Rainbow opener
Bloody muscleman
Love his pants
Human devils
Guy standing on ledge

139
Undertow
Sperm explosion
Massive bruising
Slug with blue lips and briefcase
Testerical bluebirds

140
Little girl on a curling horse
Sunlight calling through a stormy cloud
Deformed swimming hole
Whatever it is it is upside down!
Dance of veils

141
Aqualung
Slug with blue lips
Lost innocence - discovered sex
Spirit of Eagle
Orange nude reclines on Lovers' Leap
142
Seducing the Winter Solstice
Road kill scrapings
Sir Ian jousting
Chinese acrobats with sock puppets
Salome bleeds too

143
Pat-a-cake (patticake) with a flounder
Clown smile
Pastel tear drops
Zapped into disintegration
Pit bull winking at me

144
Hotdog with ketchup and mustard
Purple pixie
Christmas tree growing out of a witch
    doctor
Square dance with snorkels
Turtles trying to act like circus
    performers

145
Dancing paw print to paw print
Pink termite with bad attitude
Teddy bear nightmares
Seahorse riding a cat
Seal balancing a seal on his nose

146
Lounge lizard socks
Flame
Hunchback swing dancers
Noah's ark got melted
Guy laying on back

147
Dead matters
Bird volcano
Cars coming after the morning, they
    honk not
Tickles are free
Camouflaged deformity

148
Goldfish gold rush
Lemming without a cause
Steering you wrong
Canyon howling
Pineapple cuneiform

149
Winged elphinium
Fish climbing out of water
Garden party
Rider on a horse monster
Sometimes I see a dog

150
Shark going down
Coffee table with red feet
Melted mosaic / melting mosaic
Bubble gum explosion
Horse running around the earth

151
Telephone home dancing the sky
Priest backpack
I got the blues on the walk
Big package under the Christmas tree
Yoga class for squid

152
Green conger
Walking away
Spanish legs
Birds hatching
Blue fog with pink frog

153
Head hidden behind blue explosion
Egyptian women
Clown in chaos
Smiling worms dancing
Lion leaping off the mountain

154
Monkey walking
Archimedes hamster treadmill
Shadow dancers
Things I can't read
Dumb blonde fertility goddess

155
Walking away angry
Three ducks playing soccer
Aroma behind oranges
Cemetery at 1 A.M.
Violet horses

156
Turkey Trotsky
Elephant in elephant-hide lederhosen
Butterfly gangsters
What the floor sees when you dance
World pottery firing

157
Fox in a breeze
Steeplechase
Falcon flat-foot (the dance)
Cloud slaw serenade
Moon aspiring

158
My hand is purple because I got bit
Person swimming with shark
Blue gondolier
Tongue piercings
Shrimp on the Barbie Doll

159
Indiana Jones and the temple junkyard
Robot penguin
Serpent whispers to the shaman
Benedict Arnold
Dinosaur chasing his tail

160
Red dead rubber chicken disguised as a
            peacock
Ceremonial mask
Obscenes from a turkey
Cupid with conservatism
Demise of rodent Gomorrah

161
Saint Bernard dreams of balloons
I love it when you kiss my whole brain
Purpling downhill
The red run
Leap doughnuts

162
Whole bunch of women with green
            angels
Pennants
Echo of cat
Calm-bidextrous
Bluebird of Unhappiness

163
Blue whale surfer
Stepping stone to Japanese pagoda
Teddy bear nightmares
Blind mole with blue beret
Shark-eating person

164
Parson n the cab
Wings of wax
"V not N Gramma! It's Viagra for
            Grampa, Niagra for the ironing."
Cupid with conservatives
Vultures in mourning

165
Vultures in mourning
Whale leaking lust
Things dead birds eat
Brazilian shark with fruit basket
Surfer in the rinse cycle

166
Dancing with dragons
Cadaverous sodas
Witch fallout
Violent violet horses
Demon playing guitar

167
Sexual interpretation
Red chicken hand grenade
Violent violet maneater
Scarab poop
Eagle reversing

168
Undercurrent
Butterfly collage
Invisible man with green tie
Rainbow dog guarding
Now I see the face

169
What is he doing to that child???
Frozen fiesta
When the butterfly crashes
Soft spot in the pain
Pretty lady with long hair

170
Premature release
Time to clean the microwave
Purple hand petting dolphin
Family secrets under the weeping willow
People's changing motives

171
Saving buffalo
Center me
Green birds hear blue explosion
Ejection from an asteroid
Explosion at the candy factory

172
Sometimes I see a D O G
Mutant imagination
Monster with baggy eyes
Baby being looked at
Eagle rainbow dancer

173
Tear drops
Pregnant woman
Garbage wouldn't want me
Two-wheeled scooter
Gidget coming out of water

174
Heart
Tongue piercings
Brainstorms poem pebbles
Stoned embryos
Teal Trepok Carnariski

175
Knights of the square table
Man with head on fire
First great idea of the day
Peeping boy
Woman wit balloons

176
Nearly Great wall of china
Woman with long blond soul
Blue gondolier
Japanese woman with multicolored
        balloons
Clown shoe headed into the incinerator

177
Free-range brain
Jung on Viagra
Purple smile
Evolution to two legs
Loch Ness on bad hair day

178
Nightmare with a moustache
Feeding of the gods
Pineapple ideograms
Huddled before the wind
Leaping lord of dirty feet

179
Fourth of July typhoon
Nautilus
Horse over the rainbow
Heart of the indigo dream
Skunk squirrel

180
Exploding masks
Yellow lobster shishkabobbed on
        cerulean time
Beings between times
He-rows
Dog face with legs

181
Snowflake and dancing children
Slug with blue lips
Things dead birds eat
Kissing your jalapenos
Cat in a rain storm

182
Crab lizards
Teal Trepok Carnariski
Smear of blood on the morning after
     with yellow
Face of the dragon
Scene from a turkey

183
Steps up the side of the hill
Labors of a pixie
Blue mouse
This is where the dragon dropped me off
Waiting for lunch or something like him

184
Gidget coming out of water
Woman with long blond soul
Bird's head with truckin' bunny
Hair blown winds ? 2 women
Sound synching with screen saver

185
Blue riders on a green carousel
Disco dog chewing a rag
Reason for no air conditioning
Feather breath
Leaping lord of dirty feet

186
Two-year old's memory of the cemetery
Boat cut in half
Upbeat blues
There's my contours
Rainbow vulture

187
New year 1967!!
Wanda and Wendy Sue ate my heart
Rainbow dog guarding
Dancing Isadore's scarf caught in a
     wheel
Gyroscope candycane red peppermint

188
Nick Time and his dog Seymour
Panda bear
Cotton candy in the harem
Cat in a rain storm
Feeding frenzy

189
Shrimp on the barbie
Migration of the Bird Woman
For some reason it remade neat
     memories
Red streamers
Red chicken hand grenade

190
Carpal Tunnel Visions
Kokapelli dancing at night
Mismatched kitten lovers
Kokapelli
Gun

191
Fifty shapes distincted into one purple
     blob
We are all just failed human
     experiments
Prometheus declines rescue
Person swimming with sharks
Caterpillar golfer

192
Melting Mardi Gras
Blind mole with blue beret
Monkey and the monkey's mind
Women in cowboy boots
Dizzy dissolutions

193
Blue lover caressing toes
Vacuum cleaner in the snow
Two ducks playing soccer
Peeping boy
Casper goes nautical

194
This is where the dragon dropped me off
Storm of punctuation
To water or notter
Karnak incarnate
Fresh hot vanilla eclairs in my dreams

195
Slender purple lady with corns
Spirit of a dog
Unsuccessful plastic surgery
Blue ferrets jumping rope
Atomic Egg

196
Migration of the Bird Woman
Two ducks playing soccer
Writing the blues
Peacock road kill
Phoenix ladybug

197
Hummingbird feeding on sunlight
Montezuma with blue contemplates
    revenge
I want a new trial
Kangaroo elephant
God giving life to a crocodile

198
Porpoise leaps for the eagle
Echo of dancing kittens
Before the battle - bamboo forest
Black horse and red octopus
The vision Quest ends at a (distant,
    foreign . . .) Shore

199
Locusts with great reception
Bhudda's terrible-awful-really-bad day
Culinary organism
Two-year old's memory of the cemetery
Dancing with dragons

200
Teal Trepok Comoski
Porpoise leaps for the eagle
Salome
Monkey and the weasel
Sword-tail fish

Appendix B – Some Squish-Poem examples

Another New Life

Another new life
Pops into an ocean
Which is already
Full of life . . . . And
death —
Unknowing, uncaring
and
Unaware of both.

How soon
Will it discover
That the only rule is,
"There are no rules."

The trick is to find rules
        you can live with
—

Make them up as you go.

Go as far with them as you can;
Go beyond as necessary.

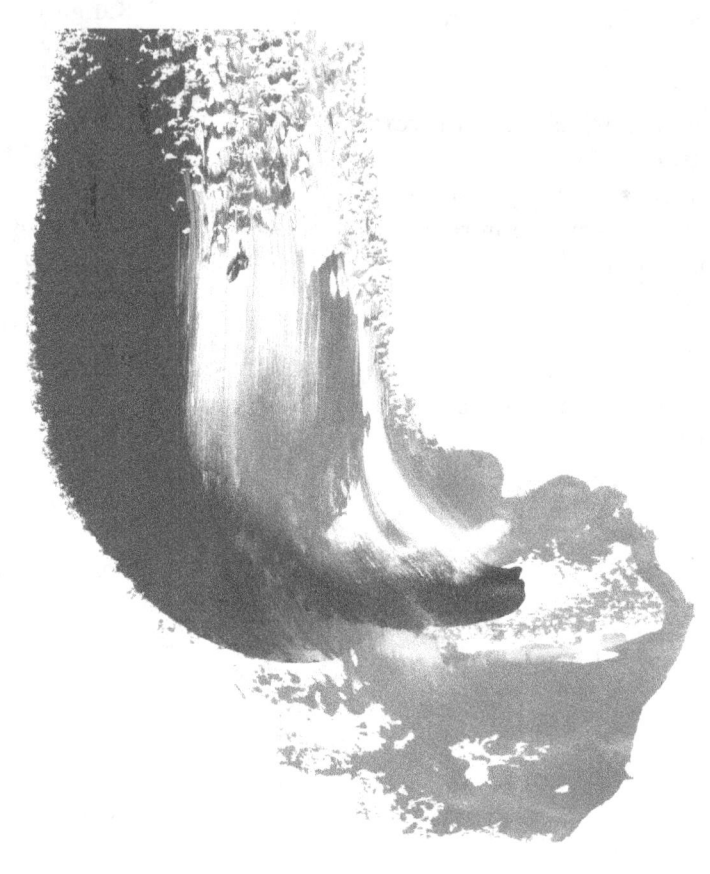

Here is another early example of Squish Art Tragic Love - 1992

Tragic Love - 1993

The Old Man of the Land
Loved the Young Woman
of the Sea
For centuries beyond reason.

One finally day
He tried to take her home
To his mountain fortress.

Her cold, yielding fluid body
Dis-integrated as he pulled her
from their mutual froth
Turning his vast mountain fortress
Into mudslide after mudslide.

He never could let her go —
They died unhappily forever after
At the mercy of Master Wind-n-Rain.

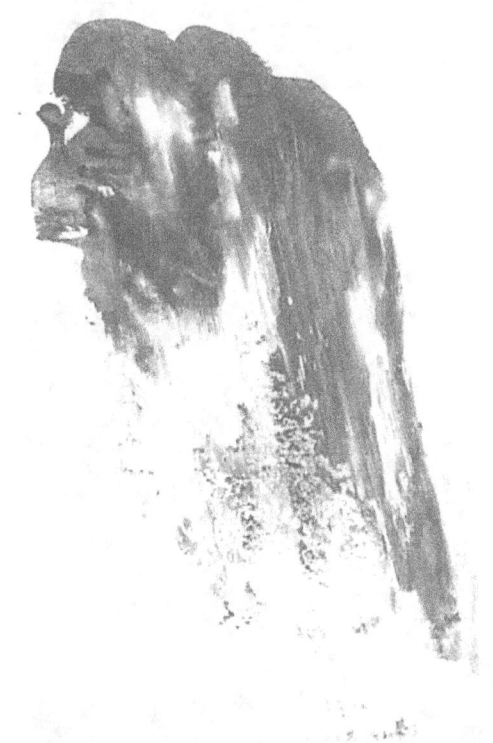

This is the poem that the picture told me. A friend who was also my
guitarist for a few years made up some music to go with the poem and
picture; we performed it together many times.

Can you see this . . . Karmic Kowboy – 1992

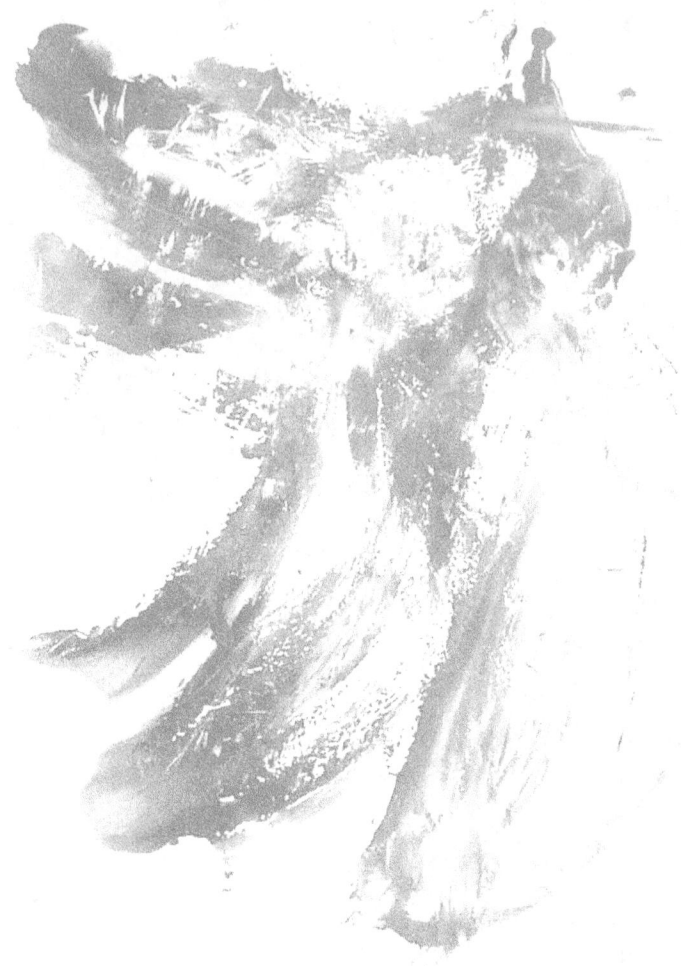

Where is this Karmic Kowboy traveling to? Traveling from?
Why? What will she/he do when it gets there?

Karmic Cowboy was one of my earliest pieces. Many folks take time
before they fully visualize the red cowboy and horse (upper right)
slouching along atop the murky seas of those many Karmic crises and
missteps that we all pile up if we ever make any moves at all.

I still return to it from time to time to remind me of all those mistakes
passed and of the bits of wisdom gained in nearly sixty eventful years.

Karmic Kowboy

So you ride your blood horse
Crost the field of life
Till you're red sore from skin to bone from the ride.

Till the you that used to be you
Tries to soar;
Tries to fly;
Tries to find the sky,
But you no longer are sure
Exactly which direction is up
Any more.

Any more than you can understand yourself enough to
        call out for the loneliness which awaits with
            open wings
Upraised like a deserted ghost town vulture;
After merely two centuries too many times that
You've been ridden wet
And put away hard.

Your are here, no?
Do something about it, yes?

Appendix C Poem Exercises

Here are a couple of other ideas generated at our house for group activities. These were generated to use as part of our Thousand Poem Party. The idea/theme of the party was to create one thousand poems in twelve hours. Although we experienced a massive thunderstorm and were rained out we generated one hundred eleven poems. It should also be noted that only about ten percent of the party-goers were accomplished poets, the rest were merely regularly intelligent and companionable people.

People Poems

Players create poems by using the words taped on their bodies and moving to create different sentences, poems, phrases, etc.

Capture the creation with the Polaroid or digital camera nearby!

Items: Painters tape, Black Markers, Polaroid camera and film or digital camera

Activities: Write a word on the tape, noun, verb, adjective, etc. Place the tape on your stomach. Repeat – it doesn't need to be the same word. Place this second tape on your back.

Gather as a group and look at the words around you.

Designate one person at a time to move people around to create the poem. Take a picture.

Scramble yourselves up and let the next person take a turn.

If only a few people are playing or for added challenge, place more than one word on a person, for example, a tape on each thigh to make a two word phrase in addition to the one on your chest. Allow poet to move them within that person only.

Try varying the heights of the people involved to create different lines in your poem. Standing, kneeling, lying, etc.

Poem Grooming

Shape existing poems into your own poem using one or more poems as basic building material.

Items: 50+ poems on separate 8.5x11 sheets, 100+ sheets of blank paper, 12+ pens of varied color, writing table & chairs

Activities: Use someone else's poem or poems as a starting point and change it to make a new poem using a method determined by rolling a six-sided die. Consult the table below:

Pruning/clipping: you can take one word from beginning or ending of any line (not both) and delete a maximum of 2 lines in the poem

Streaking: take words from first stanza and intermingle anywhere in rest of poem

Layering: you can remove any words you wish, no moving or adding

Coloring: You can only add words. No moving or removing of words is allowed.

Shampooing: use all the words; no additions or removals, but no full lines may remain as they were. Move and mix words as desired.

Weaving: Put two poems together line by line using any and only words from the same line of each poem. Each original poem must have the same number of lines. You may trade any two lines.

============

Poem Stew

> Take any one line
> From a poem you have written
>
> And rebuld another
> Poem - Story
> Or idea around it

Appendix D
Poet/Writer Inspiration note pad
Sample Notepad used for Creativity Workshops

Inspiration Pad Idea Generation Assistant

By

Hod

Published by

The Poetry Barn
1634 North Elliston-Trowbridge Road
Graytown, Ohio
USA 43432

Table of Contents

Use me
Abuse me
Just do not
Lose me

Explanation of Terms

A Poem Pebble, or Pebble, is a short idea, concept or phrase, a nugget, if you will, that you can use to help you create new connections in your thinking or writing. The more unusual the Pebble phrase the better although there is no reason why they could not be normal-ish or even clichés. Feel free to make up your own.

NOTE 1: Typically, in many workshops and in my own work, Pebbles are used in randomly chosen small groups of three to five. Choosing/using three at a time seems to give the optimum amount of dissonance to induce new connections and generate new ideas.

NOTE 2: The Pebbles provided herein are randomly chosen by a computer program from a file of Poem Pebbles generated over ten years of monthly Brainstorming Creativity Workshops and several dozen other public and private workshops with several dozens of poets, artists, musicians, family members and children of all ages using Squish Art. Squish Art is a combination of finger-painting, abstraction and Rorschach ink-blotted psychology created at our dining room table in 1994 or so that grew into this general useful writing tool.

A Scroodle, a scribbled doodle, is a dashing dashed doodle which typically looks a lot like a scribble until you look at it for a while. It is, by intent, unfinished in a drawing sense. You need to let it show itself to you. The Scroodles in this pad are titled so you can, one hopes, more quickly relate them to your chosen pebbles or respond in whatever manner moves you.

All Scroodles in this pad have been created by the author
and placed randomly.

How To Use This Pad

Are you ever:

   At a loss for creative ideas or input?

   Desiring new/different juxtapositions of ideas & concepts?

   Caught with empty time on your hands?

   Feeling blank, blocked or over-clocked?

Then simply turn to any page herein; use the Poem Pebbles and accompanying Scroodle (See Explanation of Terms on the previous page.) provided as inspiration or seed to create a poem, short story or any other creative idea, or project.

Each pad-page contains a group of several sets of five random Pebbles along with a Scroodle; use these to fill in a blank page where you write down, sketch or whatever you are inspired to do. (I strongly suggest some of all of these.)

This process is meant to get you going quickly. So take no more than five to ten minutes at first for each attempt. There is no reason why you cannot further develop ideas, writing or sketches in much more length or depth later.

Remember that this pad provides a process, a tool, but is meant to be a beginning, not an end. See the Guidelines below to get started.

Guidelines for Use of Poem Pebbles & Scroodles

First rule: use these guidelines however you can. Break all the rules;
make up new ones as you go. Shatter those; stomp them to
dusty sludge . . .

However, most folks may wish to begin with the following:
Turn to any page. Select a group of 5 Pebbles from those
listed there. Pick any 3 of those 5 Pebbles and use them to
generate a poem, idea or story.

Through practice in many workshops we have found that using three
Pebbles at a time works well. This creates enough dissonance to require
creative movement off-center, but not so bizarre-much as to cause total
brain malfunction.

Do not be limited by these Pebbles. Feel free to modify the Pebbles to
suit your poem needs. For exercise try to 'play them as they lie,' for they
do lie the sneaky little worms; they lie in your mind whispering and
gossiping about us and . . .

Get it out of your head in a poem on paper off your mind. Try using this
same method only have someone else pick out which group for you to
use and/or pick out a group for a friend to use. Use the Scroodle as
another Pebble or as its own launching point or combine it with any
group of Pebbles.

World in fire
Alberta Clipper
Dolphins kissing a seal
Skull season
When the looking glass shattered

####################################

Dolphins surfing
Red wheat
scratch me back Lamb shades
Three Kings and King Rudolph
Addle-brained Abyssinian

Almost a Cat

####################################

Storm of punctuation
Forced abortion
Bonds of mirth
The earth is glowing
A Chordian question

Dance of veils
bird feet at the bottom
Winged dolphin
Bobsled
Indiana Jones & the temple junkyard

####################################

####################################

Midnight butterfly sunspots
Winken, blinken and Aaaaargh!
Don't think of a blue horse
Hose with a cow attached
Broken wing

Hammer and sickle
Cemetery at 1 A.M.
Georgia Okeefe
Snakes mouth
Watching your house slide downhill

Horse eating the greener grass
Moon under the mountains
Abalone shell balogna
Pegasus caught
Disgusto

≠≠≠≠≠≠≠≠≠≠≠≠≠≠≠≠≠≠≠≠≠≠≠≠≠
Huddled against the wind
Eeyore with yellow blanket
The morning after
God shining on panda bear
Horse running around the earth

≠≠≠≠≠≠≠≠≠≠≠≠≠≠≠≠≠≠≠≠≠≠≠≠≠

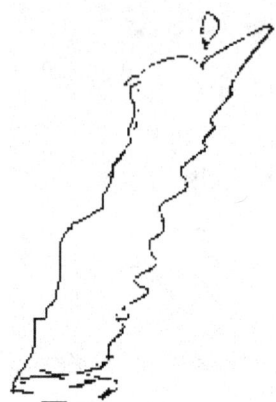

Ghost Candle

Is Benedictine green?
Blue sky eye
Boat cut in half
Eskimo water-skiing
Stoop-shouldered monk

Blue ice skates with pixie hat
Blue heron stuck in mud
Lash Larue in drag
Confusion
Moldy sharks swimming
    trudging uphill up-side down

≠≠≠≠≠≠≠≠≠≠≠≠≠≠≠≠≠≠≠≠≠≠≠≠≠   ≠≠≠≠≠≠≠≠≠≠≠≠≠≠≠≠≠≠≠≠≠≠≠≠≠≠≠

The touch of the painter's hand
Fireworks splat
Easter Island Beatles
Winged dolphin
Painting hills of copper canyon

Cabbage slaw serenade
Elephants all over
Surfeit of flight fauna
The inside of your coffee
    cup after a week without
Collision of dog, schoolbus
    and interstellar comet

Zapped into disintegration
Black horse and red octopus
Goodbye home
Bird's head with truckin' bunny
Shrimp on the BBQ

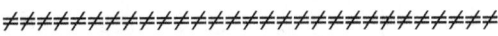

Democracy's demise
Izod eats snow cones
Lioness harvest
Marching band without tuba
Grape conga line

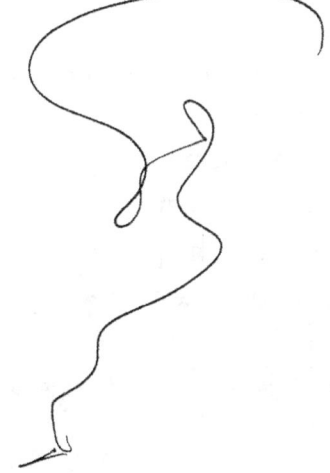

Alien Evasion

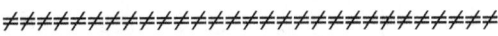

Woman with a little green gun
Imagine Lennon
Coat of mini fishes
Oxymorons for oxyidiots
Chernobyl Christmas lights

Eat my heart bitch
Swimming in fingerpaint
Bird volcano
Designed to capture
Toucan on the toilet

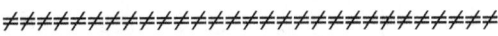

Yawning cat
A Dali-Matisse collision
Mittens and fish
Hot dog with essence of turd
Elephant in elephant-hide

Storm over the Arctic
Algae bear with algae bra
Crayola wind
Trance-fusion
Four door summer lederhosen

Montezuma with blues completes
      revenge
Bleeding parrot marriage
Angel falling into sun
Fairy circle on the green
Tug-of-war between the sages

≠≠≠≠≠≠≠≠≠≠≠≠≠≠≠≠≠≠≠≠≠≠≠≠

Things dead birds eat
Headdress
Depressed neck tie
Shark-infested waters
Pygmies dancing among the flames

Honestly, Very Happy!

≠≠≠≠≠≠≠≠≠≠≠≠≠≠≠≠≠≠≠≠≠≠≠≠

Gold rust gold rush
Water life collage
Garbage wouldn't want me
I wouldn't no
Dolphinium blue

Dripping
Iridescent seals
Melting marionettes
Orange dragonfly
Reptiles and amphibians
      reunion thingy

≠≠≠≠≠≠≠≠≠≠≠≠≠≠≠≠≠≠≠≠≠≠≠≠

≠≠≠≠≠≠≠≠≠≠≠≠≠≠≠≠≠≠≠≠≠≠≠≠≠≠≠

Horse eating the greener grass
Moon under the mountains
Abalone shell bologna
Pegasus caught
Disgusto

Cancerous summer breezes
Tossing something dirty
Elephant
Black swan in the corner
Swan rider pursued by dragons

World in fire
Alberta Clipper
Dolphins kissing a seal
Skull season
When the looking glass shattered

≠≠≠≠≠≠≠≠≠≠≠≠≠≠≠≠≠≠≠≠≠≠≠≠≠≠≠≠≠

Dolphins surfing
Red wheat
scratch me back Lamb shades
Three Kings and King Rudolph
Addle-brained Abyssinian

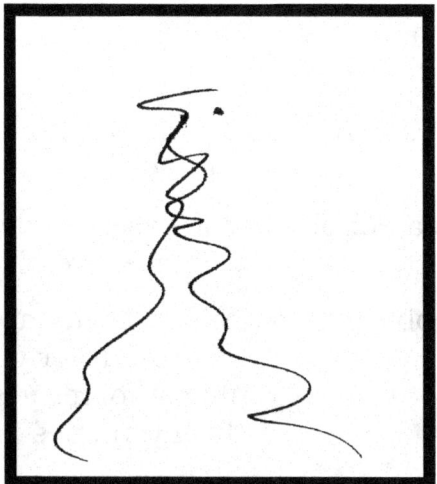

Hairy-Leg Dancer

≠≠≠≠≠≠≠≠≠≠≠≠≠≠≠≠≠≠≠≠≠≠≠≠≠≠≠≠≠≠

Storm of punctuation
Forced abortion
Bonds of mirth
the earth is glowing
A Chordian question

Dance of veils
bird feet at the bottom
Winged dolphin
Bobsled
Indiana Jones & the temple
       junkyard

≠≠≠≠≠≠≠≠≠≠≠≠≠≠≠≠≠≠≠≠≠≠≠≠≠≠   ≠≠≠≠≠≠≠≠≠≠≠≠≠≠≠≠≠≠≠≠≠≠≠≠≠≠≠≠≠

Midnight butterfly sunspots
Winken, blinken and Aaaaargh!
Don't think of a blue horse
Hose with a cow attached
Broken wing

Hammer and sickle
Cemetery at 1 A.M.
Georgia Okeefe
Snakes mouth
Watching your house
       slide downhill

Glossary

Squish Art is a simple method to enhance personal creativity using paint and paper.

Idea Pebbles are phrases or ideas captured and collected for later use in whatever creative activity you may care to use them.

Pebble group is a way of juxtaposing idea pebbles, usually random or picked out for you by another person. This allows you to, almost forces you to, come up with new ideas to connect the given ones and create a poem or story around them.

Pebble is short for idea pebble.

Scroodle is a scribbled doodle, is a dashing dashed doodle which typically looks a lot like a scribble until you look at it for a while. It is, by intent, unfinished in a drawing sense. You need to let it show itself to you. The Scroodles in this pad are titled so you can, one hopes, more quickly relate them to your chosen pebbles or respond in whatever manner moves you.

Bibliography/Resources

http://www.dickblick.com/products/liquitex-painting-knives/#photos

http://www.dickblick.com/products/logan-301s-compact-mat-cutter/

Art Supplies. Although I have not ordered anything from this site as yet I find it a good resource for comparison and general information.

(From http://www.liquitex.com/resources/faq.cfm June 2008)

Paint info. This is part of the Liquitex site and is quoted in the text.

The Art and Creative Materials Institute
1280 Main St., 2nd. Floor
PO Box 479
Hanson, MA 02341
781-293-4100 Fax 781-294-0808
This was recommended on the Liquitex site.

NAMTA (National Art Materials Trade Association)
178 Lakeview Ave 1-201-546-6400
Clifton, NJ   07011
fax 1-201-546-0393
This was recommended on the Liquitex site.

"As of May 1, 2000, the manufacturing, distribution and selling of Liquitex products was transferred from Crayola to ColArt Americas. For additional assistance regarding Liquitex fine art materials, please visit ColArt on the web at http://www.liquitex.com/ or call 1.888.422.7954 and use extension 7249."
- From the Crayola.com FAQ, May 2008,
{https://www.crayola.com/canwehelp/contact/faq_view.cfm?id=382, }.

(All addresses subject to change without notice.)